Meditations on the Essence of Christianity, and on the Religious Questions of the Day.

François Guizot

Alpha Editions

This edition published in 2022

ISBN : 9789356895034

Design and Setting By
Alpha Editions
www.alphaedis.com
Email - info@alphaedis.com

Contents

Preface.

During the last nineteen centuries, Christianity has been often assailed, and has successfully resisted every attack. Of these attacks, some have been more violent, but none more serious than that of which it is, in ***these*** days, the object.

For eighteen hundred years Christians were in turn persecutors and persecuted; Christians persecuted as Christians, Christians persecutors of every one who was not Christian—Christians mutually persecuting each other. This persecution varied, it is true, in degree of cruelty with the age and the country, as it also did in the degree of inflexibility evinced and success attained in the prosecution of its object; but whatever the diversity of state, church, or punishment, whatever the degree of severity or laxity in the application of the principle, this principle was ever the same. After having had to endure proscription and martyrdom under the imperial government of Paganism, the Christian religion lived, in its turn, under the guard of the civil law, defended by the arms of secular power.

In these days it exists in the very presence of Liberty. It has to deal with free thought,—with free discussion. It is called upon to defend, to guard itself, to prove incessantly and against every comer its moral and historical veracity, to vindicate its claims upon man's intelligence and man's soul. Roman Catholics, Protestants, or Jews, Christians or philosophers, all, at least in our country, are sheltered from every persecution; for no one without incurring the risk of ridicule could characterise as persecution the sacrifices or the inconveniences to which the expression of his opinion may occasionally subject him. To every man such expression of opinion is permitted, and can never lead to the forfeiture, on the part of any single individual, of any of his political rights or privileges. Religious Liberty—that is to say, the liberty of believing; of believing differently or of disbelieving—may be but imperfectly accepted and guaranteed as a principle in certain states; but it still is evident that it is becoming so every day more and more, and that it will eventually become the Common Law of the civilised world.

One of the circumstances that render this fact pregnant with importance is that it does not stand isolated; but holds its place in the great Intellectual and Social Revolution, which, after the fermentation and the preparation of centuries, has broken out and is in course of accomplishment in our own days. The scientific spirit, the preponderance of the democratic principle, and that of political liberty, are the essential characteristics and invincible tendencies of this revolution. These new forces may fall into enormous errors and commit enormous faults, the penalty for which they will ever dearly pay;

still they are definitively installed in modern society; the sciences will continue to develop themselves in its bosom in the full independence of their methods and of their results; the democracy will establish itself in the positions which it has conquered, and on the ground which has been opened to it; political liberty in the midst of its storms and its disappointments will still, sooner or later, cause itself to be accepted as the necessary guarantee for all the acquisitions and all the progress possible in society. These are the grand predominant facts to which all public institutions will now have to adapt themselves, and with which all authority whose action is upon the mind requires to live at peace.

Christianity also must submit to the same tests and trials. As it has surmounted all others, so also will it surmount this; its essence and origin would not be divine did they not permit it to adapt itself to all the different forms of human institutions, to serve them now as a guide, now as a support in their vicissitudes whether of adversity or prosperity. It is, however, of the most serious importance for Christians not to deceive themselves, either as to the nature of the struggle which they will have to sustain, or as to its perils and the legitimate arms which they may use to combat them. The attack directed against the Christian religion is one hotly carried on, now with a brutal fanaticism, now with a dexterous learning; at one time with the appeal to sincere convictions, and at another invoking the worst passions; some contest Christianity as false, others reject it as too exacting and imposing too much restraint; the greater part apprehend it as a tyranny. Injustice and suffering are not so soon forgotten; nor does one readily recover from the effect of terror. The memory of religious persecutions still lives, and this it is that maintains, in multitudes, whose opinions vacillate, aversion, prejudice, and a lively sentiment of alarm. Christians on their side are loth to recognise and accommodate themselves to the new order of society; every moment they are shocked, irritated, terrified by the ideas and language to which that society gives utterance. Men do not so readily pass from a state of privilege to one of community of rights—from a state of dominion to one of liberty; they do not resign themselves without a struggle to the audacious obstinacy of contradiction, to the daily necessity of resisting and conquering. Government according to principles of liberty is still more influenced by passion, and entails a necessity of still more exertion in the sphere of religion than of civil politics: believers find it still more difficult to support incredulity than governments to bear with oppositions; and, nevertheless, these themselves are forced to do so, and can only find in free discussion and in the full exercise of their peculiar liberties the force which they require to rise above their perilous condition, and reduce—not to silence, for that is impossible, but to an idle warfare—their inveterate enemies.

To leave that civil society, in which the different sects of religion are now-a-days compelled to live in peace and side by side, and to enter religious society itself, the Christian Church of our days:—what is its actual position with respect to these grand questions which it has to discuss with the spirit of human liberty and audacity? Does it comprehend properly, does it suitably carry on the warfare in which it is engaged? Does it tend in its proceedings to a re-establishment of a real peace, and active harmonious relations between itself and that general society in the midst of which it is living?

I say ***Christian Church***. It is, in effect, the whole Church of Christ, and not such or such a church that is in these days attacked, and vitally attacked. When men deny the Supernatural World, the Inspiration of the Scriptures, and the Divinity of Jesus Christ, they really assail the whole body of Christians—Romanists, Protestants or Greeks: they are virtually destroying the foundations of faith in all the belief of Christians, what ever their particular difference of religious opinion or forms of ecclesiastical government.. It is by faith that all Christian Churches live; there is no form of government, monarchical or republican, concentrated or diffused, that suffices to maintain a church; there is no authority so strong, no liberty so broad, as to be able in a religious society to dispense with the necessity of faith. For what is it that unites in a church if it is not faith? Faith is the bond of souls. When then the foundations of their common faith are attacked, the differences existing between Christian Churches upon special questions, or the diversities of their organization or government, become secondary interests; it is from a common peril that they have to defend themselves; or they must reconcile themselves to see dried up the common source from which they all derive sustenance and life.

I fear that the sentiment of this common peril is not, in all the Christian Churches, as clear and well defined, as deep and predominant, as their common safety requires. In presence of similar questions everywhere varied, of identical attacks everywhere directed against the vital facts and dogmas of Christianity, I dread Christians of the different communions not concentrating all their forces upon the mighty struggles in which they are, all, to engage. My dread, however, is unattended by astonishment. Although the danger is the same for all, the traditional opinions and habits, and consequently the actual dispositions, are very different. Many Romanists feel the persuasion that Faith would be saved were they only delivered from liberty of thought. Many Protestants believe that they are but employing their right of free examination, and do not lose their title to be regarded as Christians, when they are in effect abandoning the foundations and withdrawing from the source of Faith. Roman Catholicism has not sufficient reliance on its roots, and respects too much its branches; no tree exists that does not need culture and clearing in accordance with climate and season, if it is to be expected to continue to bear always good fruit; but the roots should be especially defended from every attack. Protestantism is too forgetful that it also has roots from which it cannot be separated without perishing, and that religion is not what an annual is in vegetation: a plant that men cultivate and renew at their pleasure. Whilst the Romanists dread freedom of thought too much, the Protestants on their side have too great a fear of authority. Some believe that inasmuch as religious Faith has firm and fixed points, movement and progress are incompatible with religious society; others affirm that a religious society can never have fixed points, and that religion consists in religious sentiment and individual belief. What would have become of Christianity, had it from its birth been condemned to the immobility which the former recommend; and what would become of it at the present day, were it surrendered, as the latter would have it, to the caprice of every mind, and the wind of every day?

Happily, God permits not that, at this crisis, the true principles and the true interests of the Christian Religion should remain without sufficient defenders. Romanists there are who understand their age and the new constitution of society, who accept frankly its liberty, religious and politic: it is precisely they who have most boldly testified their attachment to the faith of Rome, who have claimed with most ardor the essential liberties of their church, and defended with most energy the rights of its chief. Nor are Protestants wanting who have used with the most untiring zeal all the liberty acquired in our days by Protestantism; they have founded all those associations and originated all those undertakings which have manifested the vital energy and extended the action of the Protestant Church; they have demanded and they continue to demand, for this church, the reestablishment of its Synods, that is to say, its religious autonomy. Amongst these Protestants, where men have appeared who have not found in the Protestant Church as by law established the entire satisfaction of their convictions, they have felt no hesitation to separate from it and to found, with their own means alone, independent churches. It may be affirmed also of the Protestants that they have most largely put in practice all the rights and all the liberties of Protestantism, in the internal ordeal through which Christianity is at present passing; it is precisely they who assert most loudly the dogmas of the Christian Faith and maintain most inflexibly the authoritative rights established by law in the bosom of their church. The Liberal Romanists of the present day are the most zealous defenders of the fundamental traditions and institutions of Catholicism. The Protestants who have been the most active during the last half-century in the exercise of the liberties of Protestantism are the firmest maintainers of its doctrines and of its vital rules.

Humanly speaking, it is upon the influence exercised and to be exercised in their respective churches and on the public, by these two classes of

Christians, that depends the peaceable issue of the crisis through which Christianity is in these days passing. Our society is, doubtless, far from meriting the title of a Christian one; still it cannot be characterised as anti-Christian; considered as one vast whole, it has no hostile or general prejudice against the Christian religion: it maintains the habits, the instincts, I would willingly add the longings, of Christians; it is conscious that Christian Faith and Ordinance serve powerfully its interests with respect to order and peace; the fanatical opponents of Christianity exercise upon it far more disquieting than seductive influences, for it has already had experience of their empire; and where society appears to offer a silent acquiescence or even to pride itself upon them, still at bottom it dreads their progress.

Such being the state of the case, and such the constitution of society, how are we to draw men away from their apathy and their ignorance in matters of religion? How lead them back to Christianity? They alone can accomplish this object, who, in their defence and propagation of the religion of Jesus, shall not wound society itself in the ideas, sentiments, rights and interests which have at present rooted themselves in its very life and energies. Like religion, modern society has also its fixed points and its invincible tendencies: it can never be set on terms of harmony with the former unless by the concurring action of men who have with each of them a genuine and deep sentiment of sympathy. Since the Christian Religion lives in these times confronting civil liberty, those alone can be efficient champions of religion who at the same time profess fully the Christian Faith and accept with sincerity the tests of Liberty.

But in pursuing their pious and salutary enterprise, let not these liberal Christians flatter themselves with the probability of any prompt or complete success: maintain and propagate the Christian faith they may, but they will never be able in the bosom of society to get rid either of incredulity or doubt; even while combating them they must learn to endure their presence; in institutions of freedom there is essentially an intermixture of good and evil, of truth and error; contrary ideas and dispositions produce and develop themselves in it simultaneously. "Think not that I am come to send peace on earth: I came not," said Jesus to his apostles, "to send peace, but a sword." [Footnote 1] The sword of Jesus Christ, that is, Christianity, at war with human error and shortcomings; a victory, still a victory ever incomplete in an incessant struggle,—***that*** is the condition to which those must submit with resignation who, in the bosom of liberty, defend the truth of Christianity.

[Footnote 1: Matthew x. 34.]

Were these valiant and intelligent champions of the faith of Jesus not adopted and accredited as such in the churches to which they belong; did the Church of Rome furnish ground for thinking her essentially hostile to the fundamental principles and rights of modern society, and that she only tolerates them as Moses tolerated divorce amongst the Jews, "because of the hardness of their heart"; and, on the other hand, did the rejectors of the Supernatural, of the Inspiration of the Scriptures, and of the Divinity of Jesus Christ, predominate in the bosom of Protestantism; and finally, did the latter then become nought but a hesitating system of philosophy; if all these deplorable things were to be realised, I am far from thinking that, owing to such faults, such disasters, the religion of Christ would vanish from the world and definitively withdraw from men its light and its support: the destinies of religion are far above human errors; but still, beyond all doubt, for mankind to be turned back from them, and for the light to return to their soul and harmony to modern society, there would have again to burst out in the human soul and in society one of those immense troubles, one of those revolutionary whirlwinds, whose evils man is compelled actually to undergo before he can derive benefit from its lessons.

On the point of addressing myself to questions more profound and of a less transitory nature, I content myself with having merely indicated what I think of the crisis that agitates Christendom at the present day, as also of its main cause, its perils, and the chances, good or bad, that it holds out for the future. In the work of which the first part is now before the public, I omit all the circumstantial facts and details as well as the discussions that grow out of them, and it is only with the Christian Religion as it is in itself, with its fundamental belief and its reasonableness, that I occupy myself; it has been my purpose to illustrate the truth of Christianity by contrasting it with the systems and the doubts that men set in array against it. It is my intention to avoid all direct and personal polemics; express reference to individuals embarrasses and envenoms all questions in controversy, and gives rise to ill-judged deference or unjust invective, two descriptions of falsity for which alike I feel no sympathy: let me have then for adversaries ideas alone; and whatever these may be, I admit beforehand the possibility of sincerity on the part of those that prefer them. Without this admission all serious discussion is out of the question; and neither the intellectual enormity of the error, nor its awful practical consequences, positively precludes sincerity on the part of him that promulgates it. The mind of man is still more easily led astray than his heart, and is still more egotistical; after having once conceived and expressed an idea, it attaches itself to it as to its own offspring, takes a pride in imprisoning itself in it, as if it were so taking possession of the pure and entire truth.

These ***Meditations*** will be divided into four series. In the first, which forms this volume, I explain and establish what constitutes, in my opinion, the essence of the Christian religion; that is to say, what those natural problems are, that correspond with the fundamental dogmas that offer their solution, the supernatural facts upon which these same dogmas repose—Creation, Revelation, the Inspiration of the Scriptures, God according to the Biblical account, and Jesus according to the Gospel narrative. Next to the Essence of the Christian religion comes its history; and this will be the subject of a second series of ***Meditations***, in which I shall examine the authenticity of the Scriptures, the primary causes of the foundation of Christianity, Christian Faith, as it has always existed throughout its different ages and in spite of all its vicissitudes; the great religious crisis in the sixteenth century which divided the Church and Europe between Roman Catholicism and Protestantism; finally those different anti-Christian crises, which at different epochs and in different countries have set in question and imperilled Christianity itself, but which dangers it has ever surmounted. The third ***Meditation*** will be consecrated to the study of the actual state of the Christian religion, its internal and external condition: I shall retrace the regeneration of Christianity which occurred amongst us at the commencement of the nineteenth century, both in the Church of Rome and in the Protestant churches; the impulse imparted to it at the same epoch by the Spiritualistic Philosophy that then began again to flourish, and the movement in the contrary direction which showed itself very remarkably soon afterwards in the resurrection of Materialism, of Pantheism, of Scepticism, and in works of historical criticism. I shall attempt to determine the idea, and consequently, in my opinion, the fundamental error of these different systems, the avowed and active enemies of Christianity. Finally, in the fourth series of these ***Meditations*** I shall endeavour to discriminate and to characterise the future destiny of the Christian religion, and to indicate by what course it is called upon to conquer completely and to sway morally this little corner of the universe termed by us our earth, in which unfold themselves the designs and power of God, just as, doubtless, they do in an infinity of worlds unknown to us.

I have passed thirty-five years of my life in struggling, on a bustling arena, for the establishment of political liberty and the maintenance of order as established by law. I have learnt, in the labours and trials of this struggle, the real worth of Christian Faith and of Christian Liberty. God permits me, in the repose of my retreat, to consecrate to their cause what remains to me of life and of strength. It is the most salutary favour and the greatest honour that I can receive from His goodness.

Guizot.
Val-Richer, ***June***, 1864.

First Meditation.
Natural Problems.

From the very origin of the human race, wherever man has existed, or still exists, certain questions have peculiarly and irresistibly fixed his attention, and they continue to do so at the present hour. This arises not alone from a feeling of natural curiosity, or the ardent thirst for knowledge, but from a deeper and more powerful motive: the destiny of man is intimately involved in these questions; they contain the secret not only of all that he sees around him, but of his own being; and when he aspires to solve them, it is not merely because he desires to understand the spectacle of which he is a beholder, but because he feels, and is conscious of being himself an actor in the great drama of existence, and because he seeks to ascertain his own part there, and comprehend his own destiny. His present conduct and his future lot are as much at issue as the satisfaction of his thought. These great problems are, for man, not questions of science, but questions of life: in considering them he feels himself compelled to say, with Hamlet, "To be or not to be, that is the question."

Whence does the world proceed, and whence does man appear in the midst of it? What is the origin of each, and whither does each tend? What are their beginning and their end? Laws there are which govern them;—is there a legislator? Under the empire of these laws, man feels and calls himself free: is he so in reality? How is his liberty compatible with the laws which govern him and the world? Is he a passive instrument of fate, or a responsible agent? What are the ties and relations which connect him with the Legislator of the world?

The world and man himself present a strange and painful spectacle. Good and evil, both moral and physical, order and disorder, joy and sorrow, are here intimately blended and yet in continual antagonism. Whence come this commingling and this strife? Is good or is evil the condition and the law of man and of the world? If good, how then has evil found admission? Wherefore suffering and death? Why this moral disorder?—the calamities which so frequently befall the good, and the prosperity, so abhorrent to our feelings, which attends the wicked? Is this the normal and definitive state of man and of the world?

Man is conscious that he is at the same time great and little, strong and feeble, powerful and impotent. He finds in himself matter for admiration and for love, and yet he suffices not to himself in any respect; he seeks an aid, a support, beyond and above himself: he asks, he invokes, he prays. What mean these inward disquietudes,—these alternate impulses of pride and weakness? Have they, or not, a meaning and an object? Why prayer?

Such are the natural problems, now dimly felt, now clearly defined, which in all ages and among all nations, in every form and in every degree of civilization, by instinct or by reflexion, have arisen, and still arise, in the human mind. I indicate only the greatest, the most apparent: I might recall many others which are connected with them.

Not only are these problems natural to man; they appertain to him alone; they are his peculiar privilege. Man alone, among all creatures known to us, perceives and states them, and feels himself imperiously called upon to solve them. I borrow the following admirable observations from M. de Châteaubriand:—"Why does not the ox as I do? It can lie down upon the grass, raise its head toward heaven, and in its lowings call upon that unknown Being who fills this immensity of space. But no: content with the turf on which it tramples, it interrogates not those suns in the firmament above, which are the grand evidence of the existence of God. Animals are not troubled with those hopes which fill the heart of man; the spot on which they tread yields them all the happiness of which they are susceptible; a little grass satisfies the sheep; a little blood gluts the tiger. The only creature that looks beyond himself, and is not all in all to himself, is man." [Footnote 2]

[Footnote 2: Genie du Christianisme, vol. i. p. 208, edit, of 1831.]

From these problems, natural and peculiar to man, all religions have sprung. The object of them all is to satisfy man's thirst for their solution. As these problems are the source of religion, the solutions they receive are its substance and foundation. There prevails in our days a very general tendency to regard religion as consisting essentially—I might say wholly—in religious sentiment, in those lofty and vague aspirations which are termed the poetry of the soul, beyond and above the realities of life. Through the religious sentiment, the soul enters into relation with the Divine order of things; and this relation, of a wholly personal and intimate character, independent of all positive dogma, of any organized Church, is deemed to be all-sufficient for man, the true and needful religion.

Unquestionably the religious sentiment, the intimate and personal relation of the soul with the Divine order, is essential and necessary to religion; but religion is more than this—much more. The human soul is not to be divided and restricted to certain faculties selected and exalted, whilst the rest are condemned to slumber. Man is not a mere sensitive and poetic being, aspiring to rise above the present and material world by love and imagination: he not only feels, but he thinks; he requires to know and believe as well as love; it is not enough that his soul should be capable of emotion and aspiration; he requires that it should be fixed, and rest upon convictions in harmony with his emotions. This it is that man seeks in religion; he requires something more than a pure and noble rapture; he requires enlightenment, as well as sympathy. But if the moral problems that beset his thought are not solved, what he experiences may be poetry,—it is not religion.

I cannot contemplate unmoved the troubles of men of lofty minds, seeking in the religious sentiment alone a refuge against doubt and impiety. It is well to preserve, in the shipwreck of faith and the chaos of thought, the great instincts of our nature, and not to lose sight of the sublime requirements which remain unsatisfied. I know not to what extent, men of eminent minds may thus compensate, by their sincerity and fervour of sentiment, for the void in their belief; but let them not deceive themselves; barren aspirations and specious doubts satisfy a man as little as to his future spiritual interests as with respect to his condition in the present life; the natural problems to which I have alluded will ever be the great weight pressing upon the soul, and religious sentiment will never alone suffice to be the religion of mankind.

Besides this apotheosis of religious sentiment, some at the present day have essayed a different, a more serious and more daring theory. Far from sounding the natural problems to which religions correspond, schools of philosophy, occupying a prominent intellectual position,—the Pantheistic School, and the so-called Positive School,—suppress and deny them altogether. In their view, the world has existed, of itself, from all eternity, as have the laws also by which it is sustained and developed. In their elementary principles, and taken altogether, all things have ever been what they now are, and what they will ever continue to be. There is no mystery in this universe; there exist only facts and laws, naturally and necessarily linked together; and these furnish the field for human science, which, although incomplete, is yet indefinitely progressive, in its power as well as in its operations.

According to these views, Divine Providence and human liberty, the origin of evil, the commingling and the strife of good and evil in the world, and in man, the imperfection of the present order of things, and the destiny of man, the prospect of the re-establishment of order in the future—these are all mere dreams, freaks of man's thought: no such questions indeed exist, inasmuch as the world is eternal, it is in its actual state complete, normal, and definitive, though at the same time progressive. The remedy for the moral and physical evils which afflict mankind, must then be sought, not in any power superior to the world, but simply in the progress of the sciences and the advance of human enlightenment.

I shall not here discuss this system; I do not even qualify it by its true name; I merely recapitulate its tenets. But, at the first and simple aspect, what contempt does it manifest of the spontaneous and universal instincts of man! What heedlessness of the facts which fill and never cease to characterize the universal history of the human race!

Nevertheless to this we are come: not a solution, but the negation of the natural problems, which irresistibly occupy the human soul, is presented to man for his full satisfaction and repose. Let him follow the mathematical or physical sciences; let him be a mechanician, chemist, critic, novelist, or poet; but let him not enter upon what is termed the sphere of religious and theological inquiry: here are no real questions to solve, nought to investigate, nothing to do,—nothing to expect,—absolutely nothing.

Second Meditation.
Christian Dogmas.

The Christian religion knows man better, and treats man better: it has other answers to his questions; and it is between the absolute negation of the problems of religion and the Christian solution of these problems that the discussion lies at the present day.

Some words there are which we now regard with distrust and alarm: we suspect their masking illegitimate pretensions and tyranny. Such, in our days, has been the lot of the word ***dogma***. To many this word imparts an imperious necessity to believe, at once offending and disquieting. Singular contrast! On all sides we seek for principles, and we take alarm at dogmas.

This sentiment, however absurd in itself, is in no way strange; Christian dogmas have served as motive and pretext for so much iniquity, so many acts of oppression and cruelty, that their very name has become tainted and suspected. The word bears the penalty of the reminiscences which it awakens: and justly. All attacks upon the liberty of conscience, all employment of force to extirpate or to impose religious belief, is, and ever has been, an iniquitous and tyrannical act. All powers, all parties, all churches, have held such acts to be not only permissible, but enjoined by the Divine Law: all have deemed it not merely their right, but their duty, to prevent and to punish by law and human force, error in matters of religion. They may all allege in excuse, the sincerity of their belief in the legitimacy of this usurpation. The usurpation is not the less enormous and fatal, and perhaps indeed it is, of all human usurpations, the one which has inflicted on men the most odious torments and the grossest errors. It will constitute the glory of our time to have discarded this pretension: nevertheless it yet exists, with persistency, in certain states, in certain laws, in certain recesses of the human soul and of Christian society; and there is, and ever will be, need to watch and to combat it, to render its banishment unconditional and without appeal. Subdued, however, it is: civil freedom in matters of faith and religious life has become a fundamental principle of civilization and of law. These questions, affecting the relations of man to God, are no longer discussed or adjusted in the arena and by a recourse to the hand of political and executive power; but they are transported to the sphere of the intellect and left to the uncontrolled working of the mind itself.

But again, in this sphere of the intellect, these questions still start up and call loudly for their peculiar solution—that is, for the fundamental facts and ideas, the principles in effect which their nature requires. The Christian religion has its own principles, which constitute the rational basis of the faith it inculcates and the life which it enjoins. These are termed its dogmas. The Christian dogmas are the principles of the Christian religion, and the Christian solutions of the problems of natural religion.

Let men of a serious mind, who have not entirely rejected the Christian religion, and who still admire it, whilst denying its fundamental dogmas, beware of this: the flowers whose perfume captivates them will quickly fade, the fruits they delight in will soon cease to grow when the axe shall have been applied to the roots of the tree that bears them.

For myself, arrived at the term of a long life, one of labour, of reflection, and of trials,—of trials in thought as well as in action,—I am convinced that, the Christian dogmas are the legitimate and satisfactory solutions of those religious problems which, as I have said, nature suggests and man carries in his own breast, and from which he cannot escape.

I beg, at the outset, Theologians, whether Catholic or Protestant, to pardon me. I have no design to cite or to explain, or to maintain, all the various doctrinal points, all the articles of faith, which have been included in the term of Christian dogmas. During eighteen centuries, Christian theology has very often ventured to advance out of and beyond the limits of the Christian religion: man has confounded his own labours with the work of God. It is the natural consequence of the union of human activity and human imperfection. This same result may be traced throughout the history of the world, especially in the history of the society and religion upon which God has grafted the Christian religion.

At the time when God raised up Jesus Christ among the Jews, the faith and the law of the Jews were no longer solely and purely the faith and law which God had given to them by Moses: the Pharisees, the Sadducees, and many others, had essentially modified, enlarged, and altered both. Christianity too has had its Pharisees and its Sadducees; in its turn it has been made to feel the workings of human thought and the influence of human passions on its Divine revelation. I cannot recognize, in all the uncertain fruits of these labours, the claim to the title of Christian dogmas. Nevertheless I have no intention here to specify particularly and to combat such tenets in the Church and in Christian theology, as I can neither accept nor defend. It is not for me—and I venture to say, it is not for any Christian—to scan critically the interior of the Edifice, at a moment when its foundations are ardently attacked. Far rather I prefer to rally in a common defence all who abide within its walls. I shall here allude only to the dogmas common to them all, which I sum up in these terms:—The Creation, Providence, Original Sin, the Incarnation, and the Redemption. These constitute the essence of the Christian religion, and all who believe in these dogmas I hold to be Christians.

One leading and common characteristic in these dogmas strikes me at the outset: they deal frankly with the religious problems natural to and inherent in man, and offer at once the solution. The dogma of Creation attests the existence of God, as Creator and Legislator, and it attests also the link which unites man with God. The dogma of Providence explains and justifies prayer, that instinctive recourse of man to the living God, to that supreme Power which is ever present with him in life, and which influences his destiny. The dogma of Original Sin accounts for the presence of evil and disorder in mankind and in the world. The dogmas of the Incarnation and of Redemption, rescue man from the consequences of evil, and open to him a prospect in another life of the re-establishment of order. Unquestionably, the system is grand, complete, well connected, and forcible: it answers to the requirements of the human soul, removes the burden which oppresses it, imparts the strength which it needs, and the satisfaction to which it aspires. Has it a rightful claim to all this power? Is its influence legitimate, as well as efficacious?

In my own mind I have borne the burthen of the objections to the Christian system, and to each of its essential dogmas; I have experienced the anxieties of doubt: I shall state how I have escaped from doubt, and the ground upon which my convictions have been founded.

I. Creation.

The only serious opponents of the dogma of the Creation are those who maintain that the universe, the earth, the man upon the earth, have existed from all eternity, and, collectively, in the state in which they now are. No one however can hold this language, to which facts are invincibly opposed. How many ages man has existed on the earth, is a question that has been largely discussed, and is still under discussion. The inquiry in no way affects the dogma of the Creation itself: it is a certain and recognized fact, that man has not always existed on the earth, and that the earth has for long periods undergone different changes incompatible with man's existence. Man therefore had a beginning: man has come upon the earth. How has he come there?

Here the opponents of the dogma of Creation are divided: some uphold the theory of spontaneous generation; others, the transformation of species. According to one party, matter possesses, under certain circumstances and by the simple development of its own proper power, the faculty of creating animated beings. According to others, the different species of animated beings which still exist, or have existed at various epochs and in the different conditions of the earth, are derived from a small number of primitive types, which have possessed, through the lapse of millions and thousands of millions of ages, the power of developing and perfecting themselves, so as to gain admission, through transformation, into higher species. Hence they conclude, with more or less hesitation, that the human race is the result of a transformation, or a series of transformations.

The attempt to establish the theory of spontaneous production dates from a remote period. Science has ever baffled it: the more its observations have been exact and profound, the more have they refuted the hypothesis of the innate creative power of matter. This result has been again recently established by the attentive examination of men of eminent scientific attainments, within and without the walls of the Academy of Sciences. But were it even otherwise,—could the advocates of the theory of spontaneous production refer to experiments hitherto irrefutable, these would furnish no better explanation of the first appearance of man upon earth, and I should retain my right to repeat here what I have advanced elsewhere on this subject:[Footnote 3]—

> [Footnote 3: L'Eglise et la Société Chrétienne en 1861, p. 27.]

"Such a mode of generation cannot, nor ever could, produce any but infant beings, in the first hour and in the first state of incipient life. It has, I believe, never been asserted, nor will any person ever affirm, that, by spontaneous generation, man— that is to say, man and woman, the human couple—can have issued, or that they have issued at any period, from matter, of full form and stature, in possession of all their powers and faculties, as Greek paganism represented Minerva issuing from the brain of Jupiter. Yet it is only upon this supposition, that man, appearing for the first time upon earth, could have lived there to perpetuate his species and to found the human race. Let any one picture to himself the first man, born in a state of the earliest infancy, alive but inert, devoid of intelligence, powerless, incapable of satisfying his own wants even for a moment, trembling, sobbing, with no mother to listen to or feed him! And yet we have in this a picture of the first man, as presented by the system of spontaneous generation. It is manifestly not thus that the human race first appeared upon earth."

The system of the transformation of species is no less refuted by science than by the instincts of common sense. It rests upon no tangible fact, on no principle of scientific observation or historic tradition. All the facts ascertained, all the monuments collected in different ages and different places, respecting the existence of living species, disprove the hypothesis of their having undergone any transformation, any notable and permanent change: we meet with them a thousand, two thousand, three thousand years ago, the same as they are at the present day. In the same species the races may vary and undergo mutual changes: the species do not change; and all attempts to transform them artificially, by crossings with allied species, have only resulted in modifications, which, after two or three generations, have been struck with barrenness, as if to attest the impotence of man to effect, by the progressive transformation of existing species, a creation of new species. Man is not an ape transformed and perfected by some dim imperceptible fermentation of the elements of nature and by the operation of ages: this assumed explanation of the origin of the human species is a mere vague hypothesis, the fruit of an imagination ill comprehending the spectacle that nature presents, and therefore easily seduced to form ingenious conjectures: these their authors sow in the stream of events unknown and of time infinite, and trust to them for the realization of their dreams. The principle of the fundamental diversity and the permanence of species—firmly upheld by M. Cuvier, M. Flourens, M. Coste, M. Quatrefages, and by all exact observers of facts—remains dominant in science as in reality. [Footnote 4]

[Footnote 4: Cuvier—Discours sur les Révolutions du Globe, pp. 117, 120, 124 (edit. 1825); Flourens—Ontologie Naturelle, pp. 10-87 (1861); Journal des Savants (October, November, and December, 1863); three articles on the work of Ch. Darwin, On the Origin of Species and the Laws of Progress among Organised Beings; Coste—Histoire Générale et Particulière du Développement des Corps Organisés; Discours Préliminaire, vol. i. p. 23; Quatrefages—Metamorphoses de l'Homme et des Animaux, p. 225 (1862); and his articles On the Unity of the Human Species, published in the "Revue des Deux Mondes," in 1860 and 1861, and collected in one volume (1861).]

Besides these vain attempts to supersede God the Creator, and to explain by the inherent and progressive power of matter, the origin of man and of the world, the Christian dogma of Creation has yet other adversaries. One party, to combat it, seizes its arms from the Bible itself, alleging the account there given of the successive facts of the creation, of which the world and man were the result; they cite and enumerate the difficulties of reconciling this account with the observations and the conclusions of science. I shall weigh the force of this class of objections in treating of the inspiration of the Holy Scriptures, of their real object and true meaning; but I at once raise the dogma of Creation above this attack,—placing it at its proper height and isolation: it is the general fact, it is the very principle of creation which constitutes the dogma; what ever may be the obscurities or the scientific difficulties presented by the biblical narrative, the principle and the general fact of the Creation remain unaffected: God the Creator does not the less remain in possession of His work. The Christian religion, in its essence, asserts and demands nothing more.

But lastly, the Christian dogma of Creation is met by the general objection raised against all the facts and all the acts which are termed supernatural: that is to say, against the existence of God as well as the dogma of Creation, against all religions in common with Christianity. Such a question requires to be considered, not with reference to any particular dogma, or with a view to defend one side only of the edifice of Christianity. This point, then, I shall presently examine frankly and in all its bearings.

II. Providence.

God the Creator is also God the Preserver. He lives, and is at the same time the source of life. The union between Him and his creature does not cease when the creature is brought into existence. The dogma of Providence is consequent upon that of Creation.

Prayer is more than the mere outburst of the desires or sorrows of the soul, seeking that satisfaction, strength, or consolation which it does not find within itself; it is the expression of a faith, instinctive or reflective, obscure or clear, wavering or steadfast, in the existence, the presence, the power, and the sympathy of the Being to whom prayer is addressed. Without a certain measure of faith and trust in God, prayer would not burst forth, or would suddenly be dried up in the soul. If faith everywhere resists, and everywhere outlives all the denials, all the doubts, and all the darkness which oppress mankind, it is that man bears within himself an imperishable consciousness of the enduring bond which connects him with God, and God with him.

Far from destroying this sentiment, experience and the spectacle of life explain and confirm it. In reflecting on his destiny, man recognises in it three different sources, and divides, so to say, into three classes the facts which make up the whole. He is conscious of being subject to events which are the consequence of laws, general, permanent, and independent of his will, but which by his intelligence he observes and comprehends. By the act of his free will he also himself creates events, of which he knows himself to be author, and these have their own consequences and enter too into the tissue of his life. Lastly, he passes through events, in his view, neither the result of those general laws from which nothing can withdraw him, nor the act of his own liberty,—events of which he perceives neither the cause, the reason, nor the author.

Man attributes this last class of events sometimes to a blind cause, which he terms chance; at another, to an intelligent and supreme intention which is in God. His mind at times revolts at the inanity of this word ***chance***, which explains and defines nothing; and he then pictures to himself a mysterious, impenetrable power, a merely necessary chain of unknown facts, to which he gives the name of fatality, destiny. To account for this obscure and accidental part of human life, which originates neither from any general and conceivable laws, nor from the free will of man himself, we must choose between fatality and Providence, chance and God.

I express my meaning without hesitation. Who ever accepts as a satisfactory explanation the theory of fatality and chance, does not truly believe in God. Whoever believes truly in God, relies upon Providence. God is not an expedient, invented to explain the first link in the chain of causation, an actor called to open by creation the drama of the world, then to relapse into a state of inert uselessness. By the very fact of his existence, God is present with his work, and sustains it. Providence is the natural and necessary development of God's existence; his constant presence and permanent action in creation. The universal and insuperable instinct which leads man to prayer, is in harmony with this great fact; he who believes in God cannot but have recourse to Him and pray to Him.

Objections are raised to the name itself of God. He acts, it is said, only by general and permanent laws: how can we implore His interference in favour of our special and exceptional desires? He is immutable, ever perfect, and ever the same: how is it conceivable that He lends Himself to the fickleness of human sentiments and wishes? The prayer which ascends to Him is forgetful of his real nature. Men have treated the attributes of God as furnishing an objection to his Providence.

This objection, so often repeated, never fails to astonish me. The majority of those who urge it, assert at the same time that God is incomprehensible, and that we cannot penetrate the secret of his nature. What then is this but to pretend to comprehend God? and by what right do they oppose his nature to his providence, if his nature is, to us, an impenetrable mystery? I refrain from reproaching them for their ambition; ambition is the privilege and the glory of man; but in retaining it, let them not overlook its legitimate limits. There is only this alternative: either man must cease to believe in God, because he cannot comprehend Him, or in effect admit his incomprehensibility, and still at the same time believe in Him. He cannot pass and repass incessantly from one system to the other, now declaring God to be incomprehensible; now speaking of Him, of his nature and his attributes, as if He were within the province of human science. Great as is the question of Providence, the one I have here to consider is still greater, for it is the question of the very existence of God; and the fundamental inquiry is to know whether He exists, or does not exist. God is at once light and mystery: in intimate relation with man, and yet beyond the limits of his knowledge. I shall presently endeavour to mark the limit at which human knowledge stops, and indicate its proper sphere; but this I at once assume as certain: whoever, believing in God and speaking of Him as incomprehensible, yet persists in endeavouring to define Him scientifically, and seeks to penetrate the mystery, which he has yet admitted, is in great risk of destroying his own belief, and of setting God aside, which is one way of denying Him.

But I leave for a moment these two simultaneous propositions, namely, the impossibility of comprehending God, and the necessity of believing in Him; and I proceed at once to that objection to the special providence of God which is drawn from the general character of the laws of nature. This objection results from confounding very different things, and overlooking a fundamental one,—the fact characteristic indeed of human nature. It is true that the providence of God presides over the order of the world which He governs by general and permanent laws: these laws would be more accurately designated by another name; they are the Will of God, continually acting upon the world, for not only the laws but the Lawgiver are there ever present. But when God created man, He created him different from the physical world; free, and a moral agent; and hence there is a fundamental difference between the action of God on the physical world, and his action on man. I shall subsequently state my opinion as to the full meaning of the expression, "Man is a free being," and as to the nature of the consequences to which it leads; for the present, I assume, as a certain and incontestable fact, this principle of human liberty,—of the free determination of man considered as a moral agent. Admitting this, it cannot be said that God governs mankind at large by general and permanent laws; for what would this be but to ignore or annul the liberty granted to man, that is to say, to misconceive and mutilate the Work of God himself. Man exercises a free determination, and in his own life actually gives birth to events which are not the result of any general and external laws. Divine Providence watches the operations of man's volition, and records the manner in which it has been exercised. It does not treat man as it deals with the stars in heaven and the waves of the ocean, which have neither thought nor will; with man it has other relations than with nature, and employs a different mode of action.

There is little wisdom in instituting comparisons between objects or facts not essentially analogous; and the idea of God has been so often disfigured by representing Him in the image of man, that I mistrust the efficacy of any analogies borrowed from humanity to convey a conception of God. I cannot, however, overlook the fact, that God has created man in his own image, nor can I absolutely refrain from seeking, in nature or the life of man, some type to shadow forth the features of God. Let us consider the human family: the father and mother assist in directing the active development of the child; they watch over it with authority and tenderness; they control its liberty without annulling it, and they listen to its little prayers—now granting them, now refusing them, as their reason dictates, and with a view to the child's main and future interests. The child, without thought or design, by the spontaneous instinct of its nature, recognizes the authority and feels the tenderness of its parents; as it advances in age, it sometimes obeys and sometimes resists their injunctions, using or misusing its natural liberty; but in all the fickleness of its will, it asks, it entreats, full of confidence—joyous and thankful when it obtains from its parents what it desires; yet, when denied, still ready again to ask and to entreat with the same confidence as before.

This is what takes place in the government of the human family when ruled according to the dictates of nature and right. An image we have here, imperfect but still true—a shadowing-forth, faint yet faithful—of Divine Providence. Thus it is that the Christian religion qualifies and describes the action of God in the life of man. It exhibits God as ever present and accessible to man, as a father to his child; it exhorts, encourages, invites man to implore, to confide in, to pray to God. It reserves absolutely the answer of God to that prayer; He will grant, or He will refuse: we cannot penetrate his motives—"The ways of God are not our ways." Nevertheless, to prayer, ceaseless and ever renewed, the Christian dogma associates the firm hope that "nothing is impossible with God." This dogma is thus in full and intimate harmony with the nature of man; whilst recognizing his liberty, it does homage to his dignity; in tendering to him the resource of an appeal to God it provides for his weakness. In science, it suppresses not the mystery which cannot be suppressed; but, in man's life, it solves the natural problem which weighs upon the soul.

III. Original Sin.

The dogmas of Creation and Providence bring us into the presence of God; it is the action of God upon the world and man that they proclaim and affirm. The dogma of Original Sin brings us back to man; it is the act of man towards God, which stands at the very beginning of the history of mankind.

In what does this dogma consist? What are the elements and the essential facts which constitute it, and upon which it is founded?

The dogma of Original Sin implies and affirms these propositions:

1. That God, in creating man, has created him an agent, moral, free, and fallible;

2. That the will of God is the moral law of man, and obedience to the will of God is the duty of man, inasmuch as he is a moral and free agent;

3. That, by an act of his own free will, man has knowingly failed in his duty, by disobeying the law of God;

4. That the free man is a responsible being, and that disobedience to the law of God has justly entailed on him punishment;

5. That that responsibility and that punishment are hereditary, and that the fault of the first man has weighed and does weigh upon the human race.

The authority of God, the duty of obedience to the law of God, the liberty and responsibility of man, the heritage of human responsibility are, in their moral chronology, the principles and the facts comprised in the dogma of Original Sin.

I turn away my attention for a moment from the dogma itself, its source, its history, the Biblical and Christian tradition of this first step in evil of the human race. And considering man, his nature, and his destiny in their actual and general state, I investigate and verify the moral facts as they manifest themselves at the present day, to the eyes of good sense, amidst the disputes of the learned.

Man, at his birth, is subjected to the moral authority, as well as the physical power of the parents who, humanly speaking, created him. Obedience is to him a duty, and at the same time a necessity. This physical necessity and this moral obligation, however ultimately connected with each other, are not one and identical; and the child, in its spontaneous development, instinctively feels the moral obligation long before it is conscious of the physical necessity. The instinctive feeling of the obligation is united with the growing sentiment of affection; and the child obeys the look, the voice of its mother, unconscious of its absolute dependence upon her. As the sentiment of affection and the instinct of obligatory obedience are the first dawn of moral good in the development of the child, so the impulse to disobedience is the first symptom, the first appearance of moral evil. It is with the voluntary disobedience of the child to the will of its mother that the moral infraction commences, and it is in disobedience that it resides. It considers neither the motives nor the consequences of its act; it is simply conscious that it disobeys, and regards its mother with a mingled feeling of restlessness and defiance; it tries, with hesitation, the maternal authority; it strives to be, and especially to appear, independent of the natural and legitimate power which rules it, and which it recognises at the very moment when it opposes its own will to that higher law.

As the child, so is the man. As man is born free, so he lives free; and as he is born subject, so he lives subject. Liberty co-exists with authority and resists without annulling it. Authority exists before liberty, and as it does not yield to it, so neither does it supersede it. Man, inasmuch as he knows that he disobeys, renders homage to authority by the very fact of his disobedience. Authority, on its side, recognizes the liberty of man, by the condemnation which it passes on him for having misused it; for he would not be responsible for his acts were he not free. In the co-existence of these two powers, authority and liberty, at one time in accordance, at another in conflict, lies the great secret of nature and of human destiny, the fundamental principle of man and of the world.

Let it be clearly understood that I speak here of the moral world, of the world of thought and of will. In the physical world there is neither authority nor liberty; there are merely certain forces, forces acting inevitably and unequally.

If the question concerned the material world, could I do better than repeat what Pascal has admirably said: "Man is but a reed—the weakest in nature—but he is a reed which thinks; the universe need not rise in arms to crush him; a vapour, a drop of water suffices to kill him. But were the universe to crush him, man would still be nobler than the power which killed him, for he knows that he dies; and of the advantage which the universe has over him, the universe knows nothing." When man obeys or disobeys, he knows just as well that authority confronts him, as that liberty of action abides with himself. He knows what he does, and he charges himself with the responsibility. Moral order is here complete.

Throughout all times and in all places, in all men, as in the first man, disobedience to legitimate authority is the principle and foundation of moral evil, or, to call it by its religious name, of sin.

Disobedience has various and complicated sources; it may spring from a thirst for independence, from ambition or presumptuous curiosity, or from giving rein to human inclinations and temptations; but, whatever its origin, disobedience is ever the essential characteristic of that free act which constitutes sin, as it is also the source of the responsibility which accompanies it.

Eminent men, eminently pious men, have combated the doctrine of human liberty; unable to reconcile it with what they term the divine prescience, they have denied the fundamental fact of the nature of man, rather than fully acknowledge the mystery of the nature of God. Others, equally eminent and sincere, have limited themselves to raising doubts regarding human liberty, and denying it the value of an absolute and peremptory fact. In my opinion, they have confounded facts essentially different, although intimately blended; they have ignored the special and simple character of the very fact of free will. During a course of lectures which I delivered thirty-five years ago at the Sorbonne, on the history of civilization in France, having occasion to examine the controversy of St. Augustine with Pelagius on free will, predestination, and grace, I explained these subjects in terms which I repeat here, finding no others which appear to me more exact and more complete:—

> "The fact which lies at the foundation of the whole dispute," I said in 1829, "is liberty, free will, the human will. To comprehend this fact exactly, we must divest it of every foreign element, and confine it strictly to itself. It is the want of this precaution that has led to such frequent misconception of the thing itself; men have not looked

simply at the fact of liberty, and at that alone. It has been viewed and described, so to speak, ***péle-méle*** with other facts, closely connected to it, it is true, in the moral life of man, but which are no less essentially different. For example, human liberty has been said to consist in the act of deliberating upon and choosing between motives; that deliberation, and that choice and judgment consequent upon it, have been regarded as the essence of free will. Not so at all. These are acts of the intellect, not of liberty; it is before the intellect that the various motives of resolution and action, interests, passions, opinions, and such like, present themselves; the intellect considers, compares, estimates, weighs, and judges them. This is a preparatory task, which precedes the act of volition, but which does not in any way constitute it. When, after deliberation, man has taken full cognisance of the motives presented to him, and of their value, there takes place a process entirely new, and wholly different, that of free will; man forms a resolution—that is to say, he commences a series of facts having their source in himself, of which he regards himself as the author; and these are effectuated because he wills them; they would have no existence did he not will it, and would be different if he desired to produce them otherwise. Now, let us imagine all remembrance of this process of intellectual deliberation obliterated, the motives so known and appreciated, forgotten; concentrate your thought, and that of the man who takes a resolution, upon the moment when he says, 'It is my will, therefore I shall do so; and ask yourself, ask too the man, whether he could not will and act otherwise. Without doubt, you will reply, as he will do, 'Assuredly,' and this it is that reveals the fact of liberty; it consists wholly in the resolution which man takes after the deliberation is at an end; it is the resolution that is the proper act of man, which is through him and through him alone; a simple act, independent of all the facts which precede or accompany it, identical in the most varied circumstances, always the same, whatever be its motives or its results.

"At the same time that man feels himself free, and is conscious of the power of commencing by his own will alone a series of facts, he recognises that his will is subjected to the empire of a certain law, which takes different names, according to the circumstances to which it is applied—moral law, reason, good sense, &c ... Man is free, but according even to man's own way of thinking, his will is not arbitrary; he may use it in an absurd, senseless, unjust, and culpable manner, and whenever he uses it a certain rule must govern it. The observance of this rule is his duty, the task assigned to his liberty."

It is that act of a will (that is to say of a will strictly brought back to its central and essential limits) acting freely in the intimate recesses of his being, which, in the case of disobedience to the law of duty, constitutes in man sin, and entails on him its responsibility.

Is this responsibility exclusively personal, and limited to the author of the act, or communicated, so to say, by contagion, and transmitted in a certain measure to his descendants?

I am still considering only actual appreciable acts, such as they produce and manifest themselves in the moral life of the human race.

We find the poetry and mythology of nearly all nations expressing the idea of an Utopian state of existence, referred to times remote and primitive, to which they assign different names, as the Golden Age, the Age of the Gods, and which they picture as an epoch when there existed no moral and physical evil in the world,—an era of peace, bliss, and innocence. This is the more remarkable, as it has no foundation, and finds no pretext in any tradition of historical times, however remote; for from the commencement of history, from the time that we can discern any trace of facts at all precise and authentic, it is not the Golden Age, on the contrary, it is the Iron Age which appears—an epoch of violence and ignorance and barbarism, in which war and force are rampant, and which has not in effect the least resemblance to those beautiful dreams of ancient poetry. Without now seeking to establish any relation between these mythological dreams and the Biblical traditions; or, for the moment, drawing from the Golden Age any argument in support of the Garden of Eden; I merely point it out as a great fact, as evidence of a general instinct, so to say, of the human imagination. What is the meaning of this? Whence comes this Utopia of innocence and bliss in the cradle of the human race? To what does this idea of a primal time, without strife, without sin, and without pain, correspond?

But from this cradle of man and this primitive poetry, to revert to the present time, to real life, to the cradle of the infant, why is it that, apart from all personal affection, we so readily term infancy the age of innocence? How is it that we find it so charming to give it this name, and regard it under this aspect? Physical ill is already present, for it begins with the very beginning of life; but moral ill has not yet appeared; life has not yet brought to the soul its trials, nor called forth its failings, and the idea of the soul without spot or stain has for us an inexpressible attraction; we feel a deep joy in witnessing innocence, or at least its image in the child, when we no longer see it around us, nor find it within ourselves.

What means this universal instinct, which in the dreams of the imagination, as well as in the intimate scenes of domestic life, whether we turn in thought to the cradle of the human race or to that of the infant, leads us to regard innocence as the primitive and normal state of man, and makes us place in the spot where innocence resides that which some term Paradise, and others the Golden Age?

Manifestly between the soul without spot and the soul tainted with evil, between the creature who is merely fallible and the creature who has sinned, there is a very great change of state, a distance immense, an abyss. We have a secret feeling of this deplorable change, of the fall into this abyss; and it is without premeditation, by the mere impulse of our nature, that we suffer our thoughts to bear us far—far beyond that abyss, and to pause on the rapturous contemplation of a state anterior to the fall. Hence spring, and thus are explained, the power and the charm which the idea of innocence has for us; absolute innocence we have never seen, but the idea is still vouchsafed to us; and so it appears to us in the cradle of the world, and in the cradle of the infant, and the pleasure is infinite which we derive from the ideal spectacle of purity which they each suggest.

Is this a pleasure foreign to all personal sentiment, to all secret reference to ourselves, the pleasure, that is to say, of a simple spectator? No: these impressions, which the picture of innocence awakens in us, are connected with and carry us back to ourselves; this change in the state of man, that mysterious Past which has thrown him so far from innocence, leaving him, nevertheless, the idea and the worship of it—these were not the lot of the first man alone: the entire human race was, and remains, subject to them. Our present evil does not proceed solely from ourselves; we have received it as a heritage before having brought it upon us as a penalty: we are not merely fallible beings, we are the children of a being who has sinned.

How can we feel surprise at this inheritance of woe! Have we not daily the example and the spectacle before our eyes? It is an incontestable and undisputed fact, that two elements enter into the moral life of man: on the one side, his innate dispositions, his natural and involuntary inclinations,—on the other, his inmost and individual will. The natural inclinations of a man do not destroy his moral liberty nor enslave his will, but they render its exercise more laborious and more difficult to him; it is not a chain which he carries, it is a burden that he bears. Equally incontestable and undisputed is it that the natural dispositions of men are different and unequally distributed; no one is entirely exempt from evil inclinations; every man is not only fallible, but prone to transgress, and prone not only to transgress, but to transgress in some particular direction or other. Nor can the fact be disputed, although appreciable with more difficulty, that the natural and special dispositions of the individual descend to him in a certain measure from his origin, and that parents transmit to their children such or such moral propensities just as they do such or such physical temperament, or such or such features. Hereditary transmission enters into the moral as well as the physical order of the world.

This inheritance must take effect, it has done so from the first days of man's existence upon earth, for man has been created complete in his whole nature. And whilst, at the same time as complete, he has been created fallible, I ask, who shall measure the distance between man fallible, but still without fault, and the first transgression? Who shall sound the depth of the fall, and of the change which it brought into the moral condition of its author? Who shall weigh the consequences of this change to the state and the moral dispositions of man's descendants? To appreciate the extent and gravity of this awful fact, of this first appearance and this first heritage of moral evil, we have but one test,—the instinct we still preserve of a state of innocence, and of the immense space which this instinct irresistibly compels us to place between native innocence and man's first transgression; but this test is unexceptionable; it dimly reveals to us, in this fatal transformation, the whole infirmity and responsibility of the human race.

An objection is raised to this as an injustice: how, it is said, can each man be responsible for a fault which he has not himself committed—for the transgression of another man, separated from himself by so many ages? I consider this objection weak and frivolous. Such an objection would attach to all the inequalities which exist among men, to the inequality of the destinies as well as that of the nature of man, to the inequality of his moral disposition as well as to that of his physical powers. The objection would attach to the solidarity of successive generations, and the controlling influence which the ideas, the acts, the destiny of each of them exert on the ideas, the acts, the destiny of those which follow it. The objection would attach to the ties which unite the child with its parents, and which are the cause of its sometimes inheriting their evil dispositions, and sometimes suffering for their faults. It is in short the general order of the world to which such an objection must apply; it is the very existence of evil, and its unequal distribution in a manner wholly independent of individual merit which assumes the character of a monstrous iniquity. And when we come to this point, that we no longer refer the source of evil to the fault and the responsibility of man, placed here on earth in a scene and period of transition and of trial, see to what alternative we are brought. We must either regard evil as natural, eternal, necessary, in the future as in the past, as the normal state of man and of the world; that is to say, we must deny God, the creation, the Divine Providence, human morality, liberty, responsibility and hope; or, on the other hand, it is to God Himself that we must impute evil, and whom we must render accountable.

The dogma of Original Sin alone relieves the human mind from this odious and unacceptable alternative: far from being in contradiction either with the history of humanity, or with the facts and instincts which constitute man's moral nature, this dogma admits, illustrates, and explains them. The fact of original sin presents nothing strange, nothing obscure; it consists essentially in disobedience to the will of God, which will is the moral law of man. This disobedience, the sin of Adam, is an act committed everywhere and every day, arising from the same causes, marked by the same characters, and attended by the same consequences as the Christian dogma assigns to it. At the present day, as in the Garden of Eden, this act is occasioned by a thirst for absolute independence, the ambitious aspirings of curiosity and pride, or weakness in the face of temptation. At the present day, as in the Garden of Eden, it produces an immense change in the inmost state of man, a change, the mere idea of which seizes upon the human soul, and disturbs it to its very depths; it transports man from the state of innocence to the state of sin. At the present day, as in the Garden of Eden, the act which produces this change involves and entails the responsibility not only of its author but of his descendants; sin is contagious in time as in space, it is transmitted, as well as diffused. The Christian dogma exhibits the first man created fallible, but born innocent; innocent at the age of man, proud in the plenitude of his faculties, not the subject of any evil and fatal heritage. All at once, for the first time, of his own will, man disobeys God. Here lies Original Sin, the same in its nature as sin at the present day, for they both consist in disobedience to the law of God, but it is the first in date in the history of man's liberty, and the human source of that evil for which the Christian religion, whilst pointing it out, offers to man the remedy and the cure.

IV. The Incarnation.

All religions have given a prominent place to the problem of existence and the origin of evil; all have attempted its solution. The good and the evil genius, Ormuzd and Ahriman among the Persians; God the Creator, God the Preserver, and God the Destroyer—Brahma, Vishnu, and Siva—in India; the Titans overwhelmed by the thunderbolts of Jove while scaling Olympus; Prometheus chained to the rock for having snatched fire from heaven; all are so many hypotheses to explain the conflict between good and evil, between order and disorder in the world and in man. But all these hypotheses are complicated, confused, and encumbered with chimeras and fables; all attribute the derivation of evil to incongruous causes, none assign any term to the conflict, nor find a remedy for the evil. The Christian religion alone clearly states and effectually solves the question; it alone imputes to man himself, and to him alone, the origin of evil; it alone represents God as intervening to raise man from his fall, and to save him from his peril.

In the course of the sixth and fifth centuries before the Christian era, a great fact appears in history; a breath of reform, religious, moral and social, arises, and spreads from east to west, among all the nations then at all progressing in the path of civilization. Notwithstanding the uncertainties of chronology, it may be said, according to the most recent and accurate researches, that Confucius in China, the Buddha Càkya-Mouni in India, Zoroaster in Persia, Pythagoras and Socrates in Greece, are all included in the limits of this epoch; [Footnote 5] men as dissimilar as they are celebrated, but who have all, in different ways and in unequal degrees, undertaken a great work of reforming both the men and the social institutions of their times.

> [Footnote 5: These researches give the following dates:—1. Confucius, from 551 to 478 B.C.; 2. Zoroaster, from 564 to 487, or from 589 to 512 B.C.; 3. Buddha Càkya-Mouni, in the seventh and sixth centuries B.C. (he died, according to Burnouf, 543 B.C.); 4. Pythagoras, from 580 to 500 B.C.; 5. Socrates, 470 to 400 or 399 B.C.]

Confucius was above all a practical moralist, skilled in observation, counsel, and discipline; Buddha Càkya-Mouni, a dreamer, and a mystical and popular preacher; Zoroaster, a legislator, religious and political; Pythagoras and Socrates, philosophers, bent upon instructing the distinguished bands of disciples whom they gathered around them. There is no doubt, notwithstanding the trials of their life, that neither power nor glory amongst their contemporaries was wanting to them. Confucius and Zoroaster were the favourites and counsellors of kings. Buddha Càkya-Mouni, himself the son of a king, became the idol of innumerable multitudes. Pythagoras and Socrates formed schools and pupils who were an honour to the human mind. By their personal genius and by the excellence of some of their ideas and actions, these men have ensured themselves the admiration of all posterity. Did they act up to their teachings, and accomplish what they attempted? Did they really change the moral and social condition of nations? Did they cause humanity to make any great progress, and open to it horizons which it had not before known? By no means. Whatever fame attaches to the names of these men, whatever influence they may have exerted, what ever trace of their passage may have remained, they rather appeared to have power than really to possess it; they agitated the surface far more than they stirred the depths; they did not draw nations out of the beaten tracks in which they had lived. They did not transform souls. In considering the facts at large, and notwithstanding the political and material revolutions which they underwent, China after Confucius, India after Buddha, Persia after Zoroaster, Greece after Pythagoras and Socrates, followed in the same ways, retained the same propensities, as before. Still more, among these very different nations, stagnation was only be succeeded by decay. Where are these nations at the present day, more than two thousand years after the appearance of these glorious characters in their history? What great progress, what salutary changes, have been effected? What are they in comparison and in contact with Christian nations? Outside of Christianity there have been grand spectacles of activity and force, brilliant phenomena of genius and virtue, generous attempts at reform, learned philosophical systems, and beautiful mythological poems; no real profound or fruitful regeneration of humanity and of society.

A few ages only after these barren efforts among the great nations of the world, Jesus Christ appears among a small, obscure people, weak and despised. He Himself is weak and despised in the midst of his people; He neither possesses nor seeks any social power, any temporal means of action and of success; He collects around Him only disciples weak and despised as Himself. Not only are they weak and despised, they proclaim it themselves, and, far from being troubled at this, they glory in it, and derive from it confidence. St. Paul writes to the Corinthians: "And I, brethren, when I came to you, came not with excellency of speech or of wisdom, declaring unto you the testimony of God. For I determined not to know any thing among you, save Jesus Christ, and him crucified. And I was with you in weakness, and in fear, and in much trembling. ... Therefore I take pleasure in infirmities, in reproaches, in necessities, in persecutions, in distresses for Christ's sake; for when I am weak, then I am strong." [Footnote 6]

[Footnote 6: 1 Corinthians ii. 13; 2 Corinthians xii. 10.]

And in truth, Jesus Christ, the Master of St. Paul, is strong in his sufferings, and imparts his strength to his disciples; from his cross, He accomplishes what erewhile, in Asia and Europe, princes and philosophers, the powerful of the earth, and sages, attempted without success; He changes the moral state and the social state of the world; He pours into the souls of men new enlightenment and new powers; for all classes, for all human conditions, He prepares destinies before his advent unknown; He liberates them at the same time that He lays down rules for their guidance; He quickens them and stills them; He places the divine law and human liberty face to face, and yet still in harmony; He offers an effectual remedy for the evil which weighs upon humanity; to sin He opens the path of salvation, to unhappiness the door of hope.

Whence comes this power? What are its source and its nature? How did those who were its witnesses and instruments think and speak of it at the moment when it was manifested?

They all, unanimously, saw in Jesus Christ, God; most of them, from the first moment, suddenly moved and enlightened by his presence and his words; some, with rather more surprise and hesitation, but soon penetrated and convinced in their turn. "When Jesus came into the coasts of Cæsarea Philippi, he asked his disciples, saying, Whom do men say that I the Son of man am? And they said, Some say that thou art John the Baptist; some, Elias; and others, Jeremias, or one of the prophets. He saith unto them, But whom say ye that I am? And Simon Peter answered and said, Thou art the Christ, the son of the living God. And Jesus answered and said unto him, Blessed art thou, Simon Barjona; for flesh and blood hath not revealed it unto thee, but my Father which is in heaven." [Footnote 7] Another day, meeting with a similar instance of doubt, Jesus says to Thomas, "If ye had known me, ye should have known my Father also: and from henceforth ye know him, and have seen him. Philip saith unto him, Lord, shew us the Father, and it sufficeth us. Jesus saith unto him, Have I been so long time with you, and yet hast thou not known me, Philip? he that hath seen me hath seen the Father." [Footnote 8]

[Footnote 7: Matthew xvi. 13-17.]

[Footnote 8: John, xiv. 7-9.]

It has been remarked, that there are certain variations in the language of the Apostles, and certain shades of difference in their leading impressions; and this is indeed true: they call Jesus Christ at one time the Son of God, at another the Son of Man; they regard Him and represent Him now under his divine aspect, at another under his human aspect; they do not present exactly the same image of Him; they do not all equally dwell upon the same traits of his nature, or the same facts of his earthly life. St. Matthew is more a narrator and moralist; it is he who relates with fuller details the birth and childhood of Jesus Christ, and who gives at the greatest length the Sermon on the Mount. St. John is more in the habit of contemplating and depicting the divine nature of Jesus Christ and his relation to God: "In the beginning was the Word, and the Word was with God, and the Word was God. ... And the Word was made flesh, and dwelt amongst us, and we beheld his glory, the glory as of the only-begotten of the Father, full of grace and truth. … No man hath seen God at any time; the only-begotten Son, which is in the bosom of the Father, he hath declared him." [Footnote 9]

[Footnote 9: John, i. 1, 14, 18.]

It is also St. John who relates the testimony of the Forerunner, St. John the Baptist, answering to those who had said to him that all men come to Jesus Christ: "Ye yourselves bear me witness, that I said, I am not the Christ, but that I am sent before him. … He that cometh from above is above all. … He whom God hath sent speaketh the words of God: for God giveth not the Spirit by measure unto him. … The Father loveth the Son, and hath given all things into his hand" [Footnote 10] St. Paul is more systematic, and enters more fully into the questions and principles of the Christian doctrine, and he regards the divinity of Jesus Christ as the first of these principles. He writes to the Philippians: "Let this mind be in you, which was also in Christ Jesus: who, being in the form of God, thought it no usurpation to be equal with God: but made himself of no reputation, and took upon him the form of a servant, and was made in the likeness of men: and being found in fashion as a man, he humbled himself, and became obedient unto death, even the death of the cross." [Footnote 11]

[Footnote 10: John iii. 28, 31, 34, and 35.]

[Footnote 11: Philippians ii. 5-6. I have given this verse in Osterwald's translation, which is also that of the Vulgate; but my son Guillaume, who is following out a careful course of study of Latin and Greek philology in sacred and profane literature, reminds me that the text of this passage presents a difficulty which furnished a field for the labours of Erasmus, Cameron, Grotius, Méric Casaubon, in the sixteenth century, as well as many others before and after them. The Greek word ἁρπαγμός admits of two meanings, an active and a passive sense—it may designate the ***action of ravishing, of carrying off by force,*** or the ***object carried off***—the act of depredation, or the spoil. Substantives derived from verbs frequently waver between these two acceptations, and the word ἁρπαγή, which is merely another form of ἁρπαγμός, is unquestionably a case in point. Æschylus, Euripides, Herodotus, have employed it in the first sense; Æschylus, Euripides, Thucydides, and Polybius in the second sense. Now, in the passage of St. Paul, accordingly as one or the other sense is adopted, these words must either be translated thus: "He did not consider it a usurpation to be equal to God;" or thus, "He did not display as a trophy his equality to God;" that is to say: He did not display His equality with God as the conquerors of the earth display the spoils and booty which they have amassed; He did not make use of His divinity to reign, to triumph, to pride himself in it; He was not the Messiah whom the carnal Jews expected, a visible king and victorious in arms; but, on the contrary, "he humbled himself, and took upon him the form of a servant," etc., etc. This second interpretation seems more probable; the reasoning on which it is founded is thus more connected and flowing; and at the same time, it leaves the doctrine of the Apostle intact; it changes nothing in his conception or his conclusions. In this passage, as in many others, St. Paul likewise affirms the divinity of the Saviour whom he announces to men; and it is from this majesty, subjected to a voluntary humiliation, veiled under the form of a servant, obedient unto the death of the cross, that He presents an august example and an imperative lesson for Christians of humility and mutual support. It is thus that this interpretation has been admitted and defended by two eminent men, a scholar of the sixteenth and a theologian of the nineteenth century, both of whom were strongly attached to the dogma of the divinity of Jesus Christ—I allude to Méric Casaubon (De Verborum Usu, pp. 138-146, at the end of the letters of his father), and M. A. Vinet (Homilétique, p. 116).]

.... It is he "who is the image of the invisible God, the first-born of every creature: for by him were all things created, that are in heaven, and that are in earth, visible and invisible, whether they be thrones, or dominions, or principalities, or powers: all things were created by him, and for him: and he is before all things, and by him all things consist." [Footnote 12]

[Footnote 12: Colossians i. 15-17.]

St. Peter and St. John, in their Epistles, speak in the same terms as St. Paul. St. Peter says, "We have not followed cunningly devised fables, when we made known unto you the power and coming of our Lord Jesus Christ, but were eyewitnesses of his majesty. For he received from God the Father honour and glory, when there came such a voice to him from the excellent glory, This is my beloved Son, in whom I am well pleased; hear ye him." [Footnote 13]

[Footnote 13: 2 Peter i. 16, 17.]

St. John writes: "Whosoever denieth the Son, the same hath not the Father; but he that acknowledgeth the Son hath the Father also." [Footnote 14] "Hereby know ye the Spirit of God: every Spirit that confesseth that Jesus Christ is come in the flesh is of God; and every spirit that confesseth not that Jesus Christ is come in the flesh is not of God." [Footnote 14]

[Footnote 13: 1 John ii. 23.]

[Footnote 14: 1 John iv. 2, 3.]

Such is the language of the Apostles; such are, at the same time, its shades of variance and its harmony. They have all evidently the same conception of Jesus Christ, they have all the same faith in Him. St. Matthew, as well as St. John, St. Peter and St. Paul, alike regard Jesus Christ as at once God and man, the representative of God on earth, and the Mediator between God and men—come from God, and re-ascended unto Him as the source and centre of His being. The dogma of the Incarnation, that is to say, of the divinity of Jesus Christ, pervades the Holy Scriptures—the Gospels, the Acts of the Apostles, the Epistles of the Apostles, the writings of the first Fathers. It is the common and fixed basis, the source and essence of the Christian faith.

This was affirmed and declared by Jesus Christ himself. What His disciples believed and related of Him, is what He himself told them of himself, as well as what they themselves witnessed and thought of Him: "All things are delivered unto me of my Father: and no man knoweth the Son, but the Father: neither knoweth any man the Father, save the Son, and he to whomsoever the Son will reveal him." [Footnote 15] —"I and my Father are one." [Footnote 16]

[Footnote 15: Matthew xi. 27.]

[Footnote 16: John x. 30.]

And when He approaches the term of His mission, when, after having announced to His disciples that the hour was coming when they would be dispersed, each going his own way, leaving Him alone, Jesus Christ raises His thoughts to God and says, "Father, the hour is come; glorify thy Son, that thy Son also may glorify thee: as thou hast given him power over all flesh, that he should give eternal life to as many as thou hast given him. And this is life eternal, that they might know thee the only true God, and Jesus Christ whom thou hast sent. I have glorified thee on the earth: I have finished the work which thou gavest me to do. And now, O Father, glorify thou me with thine own self with the glory which I had with thee before the world was. I have manifested thy name unto the men which thou gavest me out of the world: thine they were, and thou gavest them me; and they have kept thy word. Now they have known that all things whatsoever thou hast given me are of thee. For I have given unto them the words which thou gavest me; and they have received them, and have known surely that I came out from thee, and they have believed that thou didst send me. I pray for them: I pray not for the world, but for them which thou hast given me; for they are thine. And all mine are thine, and thine are mine; and I am glorified in them. And now I am no more in the world, but these are in the world, and I come to thee. Holy Father, keep through thine own name those whom thou hast given me, that they may be one, as we are." [Footnote 17]

[Footnote 17: John xvii. 1-11.]

I might multiply these texts; but these surely suffice to show that the words of Jesus Christ in relation to himself, and those of His Apostles, are in perfect unison; He speaks of himself as they speak of Him; He qualifies himself as they qualify Him; He calls God His "Father," as His disciples call Him "the Son of God." He has the same faith in himself, in His nature, and in His mission, as St. Matthew, St. John, St. Peter, and St. Paul had in Him.

It is a great source of error, in the study of facts, not to know how to stop at their general and essential features, and, losing sight of these, to give prominence to partial and secondary features. On the subject of the divinity of Jesus Christ, that fundamental principle of the Christian religion, the precise meaning and import of such or such a word may be disputed; such or such an expression may be thought an interpolation, and so eliminated in any particular Gospel, in any particular Epistle; nevertheless there will always remain infinitely more than sufficient evidence of the fact that those who at the present day believe in the divinity of Jesus Christ, believe simply what the Apostles believed and said, and that the Apostles themselves only believed and said, nearly nineteen centuries ago, what Jesus Christ himself said to them.

The opponents of the dogma of the Incarnation and of the divinity of Jesus Christ disregard equally man and history, the complex elements of human nature, and the meaning of the great facts which mark the religious life of the human race.

What is man himself, but an incomplete and imperfect incarnation of God? The materialists who deny the soul, and the naturalists who deny creation, are alone consistent in rejecting the Christian dogma. All who believe in the distinction of spirit and matter, who do not believe that man is the result of the fermentation of matter, or of the transformation of species, are constrained to admit the presence in human nature of the divine element, and they must necessarily accept these words in Genesis: "God created man in his own image;" that is to say, they must acknowledge the presence of God in frail and fallible humanity.

I open the histories of all religions, of all mythologies, the most refined as well as the grossest; I find at every step the idea and the assertion of the Divine Incarnation. Brahmanism, Buddhism, Paganism, all faiths, all religious idolatries, abound in incarnations of every kind and date, primitive or successive, connected with this or that historical event, adapted to explain this or that fact, to satisfy this or that human propensity. It is the natural and universal instinct of men to picture to themselves the action of God upon the human race under the form of the incarnation of God in man.

Like all religious instincts, that of the belief in the Divine Incarnation may engender, and has engendered, the most absurd superstitions, the most extravagant hypotheses. In the same way as the natural faith in God has been the source of all idolatries, so the tendency to incarnate God in man has given rise to, and admitted, every kind of strange imagining and spurious tradition. Are we then to pronounce all divine incarnation false, every tradition of it spurious? Rather let us say that it proceeds from the infirmity of the human mind, if we see realities and mere chimeras, truths and errors, in such close proximity, if we find them calling one another by the same names and unceasingly confounding one another's attributes. The pretended incarnation of Brahma, or of Buddha, proves no more against the divinity of Jesus Christ than the adoration of idols proves against the existence of God. Jesus Christ, God and Man, has characteristics which appertain to Him alone. These have founded His power and occasioned the success of His works, a power and a success which belong to Him alone. It is not a human reformer, but God himself, who, through Jesus Christ, has accomplished what no human reformer has ever accomplished, or even conceived,—the reform of the moral and social condition of the world, the regeneration of the human soul, and the solution of the problems of human destiny. It is by these signs, by these results, that the divinity of Jesus Christ is manifested. How was the Divine Incarnation accomplished in man? Here, as in the union of the soul and the body, as in the creation, arises the mystery; but if we cannot fathom the reason of it, the fact not the less exists. When this fact has taken the form of dogma, theology has sought to explain it. In my opinion, this was a mistake; theology has obscured the fact in developing and commenting upon it. It is the fact itself of the Incarnation which constitutes the Christian faith, and which rises above all definitions and all theological controversies. To disregard this fact—to deny the divinity of Jesus Christ—is to deny, to overthrow the Christian religion, which would never have been what it is, and would never have accomplished what it has, but that the Divine Incarnation was its principle, and Jesus Christ—God and Man—its author.

V. The Redemption.

I enter into the sanctuary of the Christian faith.

God has done more than manifest himself in Jesus Christ. He has done more than place upon the earth and before men His own living image, the type of sanctity and the model of life. The Creator has accomplished, through Jesus Christ, toward man, His creature, an act of His beneficence and at the same time of His sovereign power. Jesus Christ is not only God made man to spread the divine light upon men; He is God made man to conquer and efface in man moral evil, the fruit of the sin of man. He brings not only light and law, but pardon and salvation. And it is at the price of His own suffering, of His own sacrifice, that He brings these to them. He is the type of self-devotion at the same time as of sanctity. He has submitted to be a victim in order to be a saviour. The Incarnation leads to the Cross, and the Cross to the Redemption.

Here are the supreme dogma and mystery. Here are revealed plainly the sense and the import of Christianity. By what ways did Jesus Christ penetrate the human soul to accomplish this great work? How did He win the human soul to the Christian faith, in order to snatch it from evil and to save it?

When man fails in the duty of which he recognises the law,—when he commits the wrong which he is bound to shun,—when, after sin, repentance arises within him, and a sense of the necessity of expiation is soon joined with this sentiment of repentance, the moral instinct of man teaches that repentance does not suffice to efface the fault, and that it requires to be expiated: reparation supposes suffering.

And when the religious sentiment is joined to the moral sentiment,—when man believes in God, and sees in Him the author and dispenser of the moral law, he regards himself as guilty of transgression toward God whom he has disobeyed, he feels the need of being pardoned and of being restored to the favour of the Sovereign Master whom he has offended.

Among all nations, in all religions, under all social forms, these two instincts—as to the necessity of expiation to ensue upon the fault, and the necessity of pardon to follow the transgression—appear natural and inherent in the human soul. They have been at all times and in all places, the source of a multitude of beliefs and practices; some pure and touching, others foolish and odious: these may all be briefly comprised in the single expression, ***sacrifices***. The histories of all nations, barbarous or civilized, ancient or modern, teem with sacrificial rites of every description, whether they be of a nature gross or mystical, of a performance mild or bloody; rites invented and celebrated either to expiate the sins of man, or to appease the anger of God and regain His favour.

Nor is this all; we have here to note another moral fact, not less real although it seems stranger to the eyes of superficial reason. Mankind has believed that a fault might be expiated by another than its author, that innocent victims might be efficaciously offered up to influence God, and to save the guilty. This belief has led to sacrifices no less absurd than atrocious: the pretended expiation has become an additional crime: it has at the same time been also the source of heroic acts and sublime examples of self-devotion. Both the domestic records of families and the public histories of nations have furnished us with admirable instances of innocence voluntarily offering itself as a sacrifice, taking upon itself the penalty, the suffering, the death, to expiate the sin of others, and to win from Divine Justice—now satisfied—the pardon of the offender.

And are we then to regard this merely as a pious, a generous illusion, a devotedness as vain as admirable? Yes, such is the view that all those must adopt who believe neither in Providence nor prayer, nor in the existence of any efficacious relation between the actions of man and the purposes of God; no solidarity between men, no connection between the sacrifice of him who practises the act of self-devotion, and the destiny of him who is its object. But those who have faith in the living God, in His continued presence, and His never-sleeping providence, those who believe that nothing in man, whether it be good or whether it be evil, is in vain, that every moral act bears its fruit visible or invisible, immediate or remote, such as these cannot fail to feel, to have, as it were, a presentiment, that in such self-sacrifice of the innocent for the salvation of the guilty, there exists a mysterious virtue. The secret of this it may not be given them to fathom, but it nevertheless gives life in their bosom to the hope that such sublime devotion will not fail of its object.

And now, to pass from this feeling, and from the acts of man, whose reality no one can dispute, to the corresponding dogmas of Christianity, let me, by the side of these acts of devotedness and self-sacrifice of the human creature in his innocence seeking to atone for the sins of the human creature who is guilty, place the self-devotion and the self-sacrifice of Jesus Christ, the Man-God, tendered to ransom from sin the race of mankind and to open to it the way of salvation; who is not struck by this sublime analogy? What connection and harmony between the purest, the most generous, instincts of the human soul, and the dogma of God's Redemption? I touch upon none of the questions, I enter into none of the controversies which have sprung up with respect to this dogma of Redemption; I do not weigh with a view to compare faith and works, nor do I essay to assign the part due to divine grace or to human virtue; I do not define or seek to number the elect, but I pause upon the fact itself of the Redemption by Jesus Christ, the fact upon which the dogma itself reposes. All that the most renowned heroes, the most glorious saints of humanity have striven to accomplish, in order to expiate the sins of any creature or any nation, Jesus Christ the Elect of God, the Son of God, the God-Man, came to effect for all mankind, by means of incomparable sorrow, humiliation, and sufferings. And, as was affirmed by St. Paul in the first century, and by Bossuet in the seventeenth, this very suffering, this humiliation, this martyrdom of Jesus Christ, have constituted his victory and his empire. And I would ask, what other spectacle than that of God made man to constitute himself victim—made victim to become the saviour—could have excited in the soul of mankind those outbursts of admiration, of respect, and of love, that ardent, invincible, and contagious faith, of which the Apostles and the primitive Christians have left us the evidences and the example? It was requisite that the victim and the sacrifice should be equal to the work. That work was the Christian religion, that incomparable system of facts, dogmas, precepts, promises, which, in the midst of all the doubts and all the controversies of the mind of man, have for nineteen centuries afforded satisfaction and solution to those aspirings of the human race, which nature prompts, whether they assume the form of religious instincts or religious problems.

Third Meditation.
The Supernatural.

To a system so grand, and in such profound harmony with man's own nature, an objection is made which is thought decisive; that system proclaims the Supernatural, has the Supernatural for its principle and foundation. It is objected that the Supernatural itself has no existence.

This objection is not novel, but it has at this moment in appearance assumed a more serious and formidable shape than ever. It is in the name of science itself, of all the human sciences, of the physical sciences, historical science, philosophical science, that the pretension is made that is to reduce the Supernatural to a nonentity, and to banish it from the world and from man.

The reverence that I feel for science is infinite. I would have it as free and unshackled as I would desire to see it honoured. But I would at the same time like to see it deal somewhat more rigorously and logically with itself. I would like to see it less exclusively absorbed by its own peculiar labours and occupations, its momentary successes; more careful not to forget or omit any of the ideas or any of the facts which bear upon the subject with which it deals, and for which in its solution it has still to account.

In whatever quarter, at this day, the wind may be, the abolition of the Supernatural is a difficult enterprise, for the belief in the Supernatural is a fact natural, primitive, universal, constant in the life and history of the human race. We may interrogate mankind in all times and places, in all states of society and degrees of civilization, we find it always and everywhere spontaneously believing in facts and causes beyond the sphere of this palpable world, of this living piece of mechanism termed nature. In vain do we extend, explain, amplify nature itself; the instinct of man, the instinct of human masses, has never suffered that nature to confine it: it has always sought and seen something beyond.

It is this belief—instinctive, and hitherto indestructible—which is qualified as a radical error; this universal and enduring fact in man's history it is which men seek to abolish. They go farther; they affirm that it is already abolished—that the ***people*** no longer believe in the Supernatural, and that any attempt to bring them back to it would be vain. Incredible conceit of man! What, because in a corner of the world in one day among ages brilliant progress may have been made in natural and historical science—because in the name of the sciences, and in brilliant books, the Supernatural has been combated, they proclaim the Supernatural vanquished, abolished; and we hear the judgment pronounced, not merely in the name of the learned, but of the people! Have you then completely forgotten, or have you never thoroughly comprehended, humanity and the history of humanity? Do you ignore absolutely what the people really is, and what all those nations are that cover the surface of the earth? Have you never then penetrated into those millions of souls in which the belief in the Supernatural is and abides, present and active even when the words which move their lips disown it? Are you then unconscious of the immense distance which there is between the depths and the surface of those souls, between the variable breaths which only ruffle the minds of men, and the immutable instincts which preside over their very being? True, there are, in our days, amongst the people, many fathers, mothers, children, who believe themselves incredulous, and mock scorn fully at miracles; but follow them in the intimacy of their homes, amongst the trials of their lives, how do these parents act, when their child is ill, those farmers when their crops are threatened, those sailors when they float upon the waters a prey to the tempest? They elevate their eyes to heaven, they burst forth in prayer, they invoke that Supernatural power said by you to be abolished in their very thought. By their spontaneous and irresistible acts they give to your words and to their own a striking disavowal.

But to advance a step towards you, admitted that the faith in the Supernatural is abolished; let us enter together that society and those classes to whom this moral ruin is a triumph and a vaunt. What then ensues? In the place of God's miracles, man's miracles make their appearance. They are searched for, they are called for; men are found to invent them, and to contrive them to be recognised by thousands of beholders. It is not necessary to go either far in time or wide in space to see the Supernatural of Superstition raising itself in the place of the Supernatural of Religion, and Credulity hurrying to meet Falsehood half-way.

But away with these unhealthy paroxysms of humanity; and to return to its sober and enduring history. We will admit that the instinctive belief in the Supernatural has been the source and abides the foundation of all religions, of religion in the most general sense of the word, and of essential religion. The most serious, at the same time the most perplexed, of the thinkers who in our days have approached the subject, M. Edmond Scherer, saw plainly enough that that was the question at issue, and he has so put it in the third of his "Conversations Théologiques," noble yet sad imaging forth of the fermentation in his own ideas and the struggles which they occasion in his soul. "The Supernatural is not a something external to religion," says one of the two speakers between whom M. Scherer supposes the discussion, "it is religion itself." "No," says the other, "the Supernatural is not the peculiar element of religion, but rather of superstition: the Supernatural fact has no relation with the human soul, for it is the essence of the Supernatural that it goes beyond all those conditions which constitute credibility; its essence indeed is the being ***anti-human***." The discussion continues and becomes animated: the contrary nature of the perplexities experienced by the two speakers becomes manifest. "Perhaps," says the Rationalist, "the Supernatural was a necessary form of religion for ill cultivated minds: but rightly or wrongly, our modern civilization rejects miracles; without positive denial, it remains indifferent to them. Even the preacher knows not how to deal with them; the more he is in earnest, the more his Christian feeling has inwardness and vitality, the more does the miracle also disappear from his teaching. Miracles formerly constituted the great force of the sermon, at the present day what are they but a secret source of embarrassment? Everybody feels vaguely when confronted by the marvellous accounts in our sacred volumes, what he feels when confronted by the Legends of the Saints; it is impossible for that to be religion, it is only its superfoetation." "It is true," exclaims with sorrow the hesitating Christian, "we believe no longer in miracles; you might have added that neither do we any more believe in God himself; the two things go together. We hear much now-a-days of Christian Spiritualism—of the religion of the conscience, and you yourself seem to see that men in giving up miracles are making progress in religion. Ah! why is it that the intimate experience of my own heart cannot express itself in a forcible protest against any such opinion? Whenever I find my faith in miraculous agency vacillating within me, the image of my God seems to be fading away from my eyes: He ceases to be for me God the free, the living, the personal; the God with whom the soul converses, as with a master and friend; and this holy dialogue once interrupted, what is left us? How does life become sad? how does it lose its illusions? Reduced to the satisfaction of mere physical wants, to eat, to drink, to sleep, to make money, deprived of all horizon, how puerile does our maturity appear, how sorrowful our old age, how meaningless our anxieties!

"No more mystery, no more innocence, no more infinity, no longer any heaven above our heads, no more poesy. Ah! be sure: the incredulity which rejects the miracle has a tendency to unpeople heaven, and to disenchant the earth. The Supernatural is the natural sphere of the soul. It is the essence of its faith, of its hope, of its love. I know how specious criticism is, how victorious its arguments often appear; but I know one thing besides, and perhaps I might here even appeal to your own testimony; in ceasing to believe in what is miraculous, the soul finds that it has lost the secret of divine life; henceforth it is urged downwards towards the abyss, soon it lies on the earth, and not seldom in the dirt."

In his turn the disbeliever in the Supernatural is troubled and saddened: "Listen," he says: "the history of humanity seems to be sometimes moving in obedience to the following scheme. The world begins with religion, and, referring all phenomena to a first cause, it sees God everywhere. Then comes philosophy, which, having discovered the connection of secondary causes, and the laws of their operation, makes a corresponding deduction from the direct intervention of divinity, and then founding itself upon the idea of necessity (for it is only necessity which falls within the domain of science, and science is in fact but the knowledge of what is necessary); philosophy tends in its very fundamental principle to exclude God from the world. It does more; it finishes by denying human liberty as it has denied God. The reason is evident: liberty is a cause beyond the sphere of the necessary connection of causes, a first cause, a cause which serves as cause to itself: and from that moment philosophy, unequal to any explanation, feels itself disposed to deny that first cause. A philosophy true to itself will ever be fatalistic. For from that moment philosophy corrupts and destroys itself. When it has no other God than the universe, no other man than the chief of the mammalia, what is it but a mere system of Zoology? Zoology constitutes the whole science of the epoch, of the Materialists, and to speak plainly, that is our position at the present day. But materialism can never be the be-all and the end-all of the human race. Corrupt and enervated, society is passing through immense catastrophes, is falling in ruins; the iron harrow of Revolution is breaking up mankind like the clods of the field; in the bloody furrows germinate new races; the soul in the agony of its distress believes once more; it resumes its faith in virtue, it finds again the language of prayer. To the age of the Renaissance succeeded that of the Reformation; to the Germany of Frederick the Great, the Germany of 1812. So faith springs up for ever and ever out of its ashes. Ah, that I must add it, humanity rises again but to resume the march which I have just described. But can it be said of it besides, that like this Globe of ours it is making any movement in advance whilst it is so turning round itself, and if it does so advance, towards what is it gravitating?

> 'Whither, whither, O Lord,
> marches the earth in the heavens?'" [Footnote 18]

[Footnote 18: Mélange de Critique Religieuse, par Edmond Scherer—Conversations Théologiques, pp. 169-187.]

But it is not towards heaven that the earth would march if it followed the path in which the adversaries of the Supernatural are impelling it. It is this peculiarity, they say, of the Supernatural, that being incredible, it is in its very essence anti-human. Now it is precisely to something not anti-human but superhuman that the human soul aspires, and there seeks to realize these aspirations in the Supernatural. We should be never weary of repeating it; the whole finite world in its entirety, with all its facts and all its laws, comprising indeed man himself, suffices not for the soul of man; it requires something grander and more perfect for the subject of its contemplation, the object of its love; it desires to fix its trust in something more stable; to lean upon something less fragile. This supreme and sublime ambition it is to which religion, in its widest sense, gives birth and supplies nourishment; and this supreme and sublime ambition it is also that the religion of Christ more particularly responds to and satisfies. Let those, therefore, who flatter themselves that although abolishing the belief in the Supernatural, they leave Christians still Christians, undeceive themselves; what they are abolishing, destroying, is very religion, for their arguments assail all religion in general, and Christianity in particular. It may be that they do not inflict upon themselves all this evil, and that in retaining a sincere religious sentiment they really believe themselves nearly Christians; the soul struggles against the errors of the thought, and a moral suicide is a rare spectacle. But the evil even in spreading unveils more plainly its nature and increases in intensity; besides men, in masses, draw from error far more logical conclusions than the man ever did in whom the error had its origin. The people are not the learned, neither are they philosophers, and only once succeed in destroying in them all faith in the Supernatural, and you may consider it certain that the faith in Christ must have previously disappeared. Have you well weighed all this? Have you pictured to yourself what a man, what mankind, what the soul of man, what human society itself would become if religion were in effect abolished, if religious faith entirely disappeared? I will not give way to anguish of soul or sinister presentiments, but I do not hesitate to affirm that no imagination can represent with adequate fidelity what would take place in us and around us if the place at present occupied by Christian belief were on a sudden to become vacant, and its empire annihilated. No one could pronounce to what degree of disorder and degradation humanity would be precipitated. But awful indeed would be the result if all faith in the Supernatural were extinct in the soul, and if man had in a supernatural state neither trust nor hope.

It is not my design, however, to confine myself here to the question regarded merely in its moral, practical light; I approach the Supernatural as viewed with the eyes of free and speculative reason.

It is condemned for its very name's sake. Nothing is or can be, it is said, beyond and above nature. Nature is one and complete; everything is comprised in it; in it, of necessity, all things cohere, enchain, and develop themselves.

We are here in thorough pantheism—that is to say, in absolute atheism. I do not hesitate to give to pantheism its real name. Amongst the men who at the present day declare themselves the opponents of the Supernatural, most, certainly, do not believe that they are nor do they desire to be atheists. But let me tell them that they are leading others whither they neither think nor wish themselves to go. The negation of the Supernatural, and that in the name of the unity and universality of nature, is pantheism, and pantheism is nothing more nor less than atheism. In the sequel of these Meditations, when I come to speak particularly of the actual state of the Christian religion, and of the different systems which combat it, I will in this respect justify my assertion; at present, I have to repel direct attacks upon the Supernatural—attacks less fundamental than those of pantheism, but not less serious, for in truth, whether men know it or not, and whether they mean it or not, all attacks in this warfare reach the same object, and as soon as the Supernatural is the aim it is religion itself that receives the shaft.

The fixity of the laws of nature is appealed to; that, say they, is the palpable and incontestable fact established by the experience of mankind, and upon which rests the conduct of human life. In presence of the permanent order of nature and the immutability of its laws, we cannot admit any partial, any momentary infractions; we cannot believe in the Supernatural, in miracles.

True, general and constant laws do govern nature. Are we, therefore, to affirm that those laws are necessary, and that no deviation from them is possible in nature? Who is there that does not discern an essential, an absolute difference between what is general and what is necessary? The permanence of the actual laws of nature is a fact established by experience, but it is not the only fact possible, the only fact conceivable by reason; those laws might have been other laws, they may change. Several of them have not always been what they now are, for science itself proves that the condition of the universe has been different from what it is at present; the universal and permanent order of which we form part, and in which we confide, has not always been what we now see it; it has had a beginning; the creation of the actual system of nature and of its laws is a fact as certain as the system itself is certain. And what is creation but a supernatural fact, the act of a

Power superior to the actual laws of nature, and which has power to modify them just as much as it has had power to establish them? The first of miracles is God himself.

There is a second miracle—man. I resume what I have already said; by his title as a moral being and free agent, man lives beyond and above the influence of the general and permanent laws of nature; he creates by his will effects which are not at all the necessary consequence of any pre-existent law; and those effects take their place in a system absolutely distinct and independent from the visible order which governs the universe. The moral liberty of man is a fact as certain, and natural, as the order of nature, and it is at the same time a supernatural fact—that is to say, essentially foreign to the order of nature and to its laws.

God is the being moral and free ***par excellence***, that is to say, the being excellently capable of acting as first cause beyond the influence of causation. By his title as a moral being and free agent, man is in intimate relation with God. Who shall define the possible contingencies, or fathom the mysteries of this relation? Who dare to say that God cannot modify, that He never does modify, according to his plans with respect to the moral system and to man, the laws which He has made and which He maintains in the material order of nature?

Some have hesitated absolutely to deny the possibility of supernatural facts; and so their attack is indirect. If those facts, say they, are not impossible, they are incredible, for no particular testimony of man in favour of a miracle can give a certitude equal to that which, on the opposite side, results from the experience which men have of the fixity of the laws of nature.

"It is experience only," says Hume, "which gives authority to human testimony; and it is the same experience which assures us of the laws of nature. When therefore these two kinds of experience are contrary, we have nothing to do, but subtract the one from the other, and embrace an opinion, either on one side or the other, with that assurance which arises from the remainder. But according to the principles here explained, this subtraction, with regard to all popular religions, amounts to an entire annihilation: and therefore we may establish it as a maxim, that no human testimony can have such force as to prove a miracle, and make it a just foundation for any such system of religion." [Footnote 19]

> [Footnote 19: Essays and Treatises on Several Subjects, by David Hume; Essay on Miracles, vol. iii.

p. 119-145, Bâle, 1793. [Same work, p. 91, London, 16mo, 1860.—TRANSLATOR.]]

It is in this reasoning of Hume that the opponents of miracles shut themselves up as in an impregnable fortress to refuse them all credence.

What confusion of facts and ideas! What a superficial solution of one of the grandest problems of our nature! What! a simple operation of arithmetic, with respect to two experimental observations, estimated in ciphers, is to decide the question whether the universal belief of the race of man in the Supernatural is well-founded or simply absurd; whether God only acts upon the world and upon man by laws established once for all, or whether He still continues to make, in the exercise of his power, use of his liberty! Not only does the sceptic Hume here show himself unconscious of the grandeur of the problem; he mistakes even in the motives upon which he founds his shallow conclusion; for it is not from human experience alone that human testimony draws her authority: this authority has sources more profound, and a worth anterior to experience: it is one of the natural bonds, one of the spontaneous sympathies which unite with one another men and the generations of men. Is it by virtue of experience that the child trusts to the words of its mother, that it has faith in all she tells it? The mutual trust that men repose in what they say or transmit to each other is an instinct, primitive, spontaneous, which experience confirms or shakes, sets up again or sets bounds to, but which experience does not originate.

I find in the same essay of Hume, [Footnote 20] this other passage: "The passion of surprise and wonder, arising from miracles, being an agreeable emotion, gives a sensible tendency towards the belief of those events from which it is derived."

[Footnote 20: Hume's Essay on Miracles, p. 128, ***ubi supra***.]

Thus, if we are to credit Hume, it is merely for his pleasure, for the diversion of the imaginative faculty, that man believes in the Supernatural; and beneath this impression—though real, still only of a secondary nature—which does no more than skim the surface of the human soul, the philosopher has no glimpse at all of the profound instincts and superior requisitions which have sway over him.

But why an attack of this character, so indirect and little complete? Why should Hume limit himself to the proposition that miracles can never be historically proved, instead of at once affirming the impossibility of miracles themselves? This is what the opponents of the Supernatural virtually think; and it is because they commence by regarding miracles as impossible that they apply themselves to destroy the value of the evidences by which they are supported. If the evidence which surrounds the cradle of Christianity, if the fourth, if even the tenth part of it were adduced in support of facts of a nature extra-ordinary, unexpected, or unheard of, but still not having a character positively supernatural, the proof would be accepted as unexceptionable: the facts for certain. In appearance, it is merely the proof by witnesses of the Supernatural that is contested; whereas, in reality, the very possibility of the thing is denied that is sought to be proved. The question ought to be put as it really is, instead of such a solution being offered as is a mere evasion.

Lately, however, men of logical minds and daring spirits have not hesitated to speak more frankly and plainly. "The new dogma, they say, the fundamental principle of criticism, is the negation of the Supernatural. ... Those still disposed to reject this principle have nothing to do with our books, and we, on our side, have no cause to feel disquietude at their opposition and their censure, for we do not write for them. And if this discussion is altogether avoided, it is because it is impossible to enter into it with out admitting an unacceptable proposition, viz., one which presumes that the Supernatural can in any given case be possible. [Footnote 21]

[Footnote 21: Conservation, Involution, et Positivisme, par M. Littré, Preface, p. xxvi, and following pages—M. Havet, Revue des Deux Mondes, 1 Août, 1863.]

I do not reproach the disciples of the school of Hume for having evinced greater timidity: if they attacked the Supernatural by a side way, not as being impossible in itself, but as being merely incapable of proof by human testimony, they did not do so designedly and with deceitful purpose. Let us render them more justice, and do them more honour. A prudent and an honest instinct held them back on the declivity upon which they had placed themselves; they felt that to deny even the possibility of the Supernatural, was to enter at full sail into pantheism and fatalism, that is to say, was the same thing as at once dispensing with God and doing away with the free agency of man. Their moral sense, their good sense, withheld them from any such course. The fundamental error of the adversaries of the Supernatural is that they contest it in the name of human science, and that they class the Supernatural amongst facts within the domain of science, whereas the Supernatural does not fall within that domain, and the very attempt so to treat it has led, indeed, to its being entirely rejected.

Fourth Meditation.
The Limits Of Science.

An eminent moralist, who was at the same time not only a theologian, but a philosopher well versed in the physical sciences, I mean Dr. Chalmers, professor at the University of Edinburgh, and corresponding member of the Institute of France, wrote in his work on ***Natural Theology***, a chapter entitled: ***On man's partial and limited knowledge of divine things.*** The first pages are as follows:—

> "The true modern philosophy never makes more characteristic exhibition of itself, than at the limit which separates the known from the unknown. It is there that we behold it in a twofold aspect—that of the utmost deference and respect for all the findings of experience within this limit; that, on the other hand, of the utmost disinclination and distrust for all those fancies of ingenious or plausible speculation which have their place in the ideal region beyond it. To call in the aid of a language which far surpasses our own in expressive brevity, its office is '***indagare***' rather than '***divinare***.' The products of this philosophy are copies and not creations. It may discover a system of nature, but not devise one. It proceeds first on the observation of individual facts and if these facts are ever harmonised into a system, this is only in the exercise of a more extended observation. In the work of systematising, it makes no excursion beyond the territory of actual nature—for they are the actual phenomena of nature which form the first materials of this philosophy—and they are the actual resemblances of these phenomena that form, as it were, the cementing principle, to which the goodly fabrics of modern science owe all the solidity and all the endurance that belong to them. It is this chiefly which distinguishes the philosophy of the present day from that of by-gone ages. The one was mainly an excogitative, the other mainly a descriptive process—a description however extending to the likenesses as well as to the peculiarities of things; and, by means of these likenesses, these observed likenesses alone, often realising a more glorious and magnificent harmony than was ever pictured forth by all the imaginations of all the theorists.
>
> "In the mental characteristics of this philosophy, the strength of a full-grown understanding is blended with the modesty of childhood. The ideal is sacrificed to the actual—and, however splendid or fondly cherished a hypothesis may be, yet if but one phenomenon in the real

history of nature stand in the way, it is forthwith and conclusively abandoned. To some the renunciation may be as painful as the cutting off a right hand, or the plucking out a right eye—yet, if true to the great principle of the Baconian school, it must be submitted to. With its hardy disciples one valid proof outweighs a thousand plausibilities—and the resolute firmness wherewith they bid away the speculations of fancy is only equalled by the childlike compliance wherewith they submit themselves to the lessons of experience.

"It is thus that the same principle which guides to a just and a sound philosophy in all that lies within the circle of human discovery, leads also to a most unpresuming and unpronouncing modesty in reference to all that lies beyond it. And should some new light spring up on this exterior region, should the information of its before hidden mysteries break in upon us from some quarter that was before inaccessible, it will be at once perceived (on the supposition of its being a genuine and not an illusory light) that, of all other men, they are the followers of Bacon and Newton who should pay the most unqualified respect to all its revelations. In their case it comes upon minds which are without prejudice, because on that very principle, which is most characteristic of our modern science, upon minds without preoccupation. ... The strength of his confidence in all the ascertained facts of the ***terra cognita*** is at one or in perfect harmony with the humility of his diffidence in regard to all the conceived plausibilities of the ***terra incognita***.

"And let it further be remarked of the self-denial which is laid upon us by Bacon's Philosophy, that, like all other self-denial in the cause of truth or virtue, it hath its reward. In giving ourselves up to its guidance, we have often to quit the fascinations of beautiful theory; but in exchange for them, we are at length regaled by the higher and substantial beauties of actual nature. There is a stubbornness in facts before which the specious imagination is compelled to give way; and perhaps the mind never suffers more painful laceration than when, after having vainly attempted to force nature into a compliance with her own splendid generalizations, she, on the appearance of some rebellious and impracticable phenomenon, has to practise a force upon herself—when she thus finds the goodly speculation superseded by the homely and unwelcome experience. It seemed at the outset a cruel sacrifice, when the world of speculation, with all its manageable and engaging simplicities, had to be abandoned; and on becoming the pupils of observation, we, amid the varieties of the actual world around us, felt as if bewildered, if not lost, among the perplexities of a chaos. This was a period of greatest sufferance; but it has had a glorious termination. In return for the assiduity wherewith the study of nature hath been prosecuted, she hath made a more abundant revelation of her charms. Order hath arisen out of confusion, and in the ascertained structure of the universe there are now found to be a state and a sublimity beyond all that was ever pictured by the mind in the days of her adventurous and unfettered imagination. Even viewed in the light of a noble and engaging spectacle for the fancy to dwell upon, who would ever think of comparing with the system of Newton, either that celestial machinery of Des Cartes, which was impelled by whirlpools of ether, or that still more cumbrous planetarium of cycles and epicycles which was the progeny of a remoter age? It is thus that at the commencement of the observational process there is the abjuration of beauty. But it soon reappears in another form, and brightens as we advance, and at length there arises on solid foundation, a fairer and goodlier system than ever floated in airy romance before the eye of genius. Nor is it difficult to perceive the reason of this. What we discover by observation is the product of divine imagination bodied forth by creative power into a stable and enduring reality. What we devise by our own ingenuity is but the product of human imagination. The one is the solid archetype of those conceptions which are in the mind of God: the other is the shadowy representation of those conceptions which are in the mind of man. It is just as with the labourer, who, by excavating the rubbish which hides and besets some noble architecture, does more for the gratification of our taste, than if by his unpractised hand he should attempt to regale us with plans and sketches of his own. And so the drudgery of experimental science, in exchange for that beauty whose fascinations it withstood at the outset of its career, has evolved a surpassing beauty from among the realities of truth and nature. …

"The views contemplated through the medium of observation, are found not only to have a justness in them, but to have a grace and a grandeur in them far beyond all the visions which are contemplated through the medium of fancy, or which ever regaled the fondest enthusiast in the enchanted walks of speculation and poetry. But neither the grace nor the grandeur alone would, without evidence, have secured acceptance for any opinion. It must first be made to undergo, and without ceremony, the freest treatment from human eyes and human hands. It is at one time stretched on the rack of an experiment, at another it has to pass through fiery trial in the bottom of a crucible. In another it undergoes a long questioning process among the fumes and the filtrations and the intense heat of a

> laboratory; and not till it has been subjected to all this inquisitorial torture and survived it, is it preferred to a place in the temple of Truth, or admitted among the laws and lessons of a sound philosophy."

No one certainly will contest that this is the language of a fervent disciple of science. It is impossible to have a keener apprehension of its beauty, and to accept more completely its laws. What mathematician, natural philosopher, physiologist, or chemist, could speak in terms of greater respect and submission of the necessity of observation, and of the authority of experience? Dr. Chalmers is not the less for that a true and fervent Christian; his religious faith equals his scientific exactitude: he receives Christ, and professes Christ's doctrine with as firm a voice as he does Bacon and Bacon's method. Not that for him religious belief is the mere result of education, of tradition, of habit; but it, on the contrary, springs as much from reflection and learning, as his acquirements in natural science themselves; in each sphere he has probed the very sources and weighed the motives of his convictions. How did he, in each instance, reach such a haven of repose? Whence in him this harmony between the philosopher and the Christian?

Let us again allow Dr. Chalmers to speak for himself:—

> "It is of importance here to remark that the enlargement of our knowledge in all the natural sciences, so far from adding to our presumption, should only give a profounder sense of our natural incapacity and ignorance in reference to the science of theology. It is just as if in studying the policy of some earthly monarch we had made the before unknown discovery of other empires and distant territories whereof we knew nothing but the existence and the name. This might complicate the study without making the object of it at all more comprehensible, and so of every new wonder which philosophy might lay open to the gaze of inquirers. It might give us a larger perspective of the creation than before, yet, in ***fact***, cast a deeper shade of obscurity over the counsels and ways of the Creator. We might at once obtain a deeper insight into the secrets of the workmanship, and yet feel, and legitimately feel, to be still more deeply out of reach, the secret purposes of Him who worketh all in all. Every discovery of an addition to the greatness of his works may bring with it an addition to the unsearchableness of his ways. ....
>
> "That telescope which has opened our way to suns and systems innumerable, leaves the moral administration connected with them in deepest secrecy. It has made known to us the bare existence of other worlds; but it would require another instrument of discovery ere we could understand their relation to ourselves, as products of the same Almighty Hand, as parts or members of a family under the same

paternal guardianship. This more extended survey of the Material Universe just tells us how little we know of the Moral or Spiritual Universe. It reveals nothing to us of the worlds that roll in space, but the bare elements of Motion, and Magnitude, and Number—and so leaves us at a more hopeless distance from the secret of the Divine administration than when we reasoned of the Earth as the Universe, of our species as the alone rational family of God that He had implicated with body, or placed in the midst of a corporeal system. ...

"To know that we cannot know certain things, is in itself positive knowledge, and a knowledge of the most safe and valuable nature. ... There are few services of greater value to the cause of knowledge than the delineation of its boundaries." [Footnote 22]

[Footnote 22: Chalmers's Works: Natural Theology, pp. 249-265; Glasgow.]

In holding this language, what in effect is Dr. Chalmers doing? He is separating what is finite from what is infinite, the thing created from the Creator, the world subject to government from the Sovereign that governs it; and in marking this line of demarcation, he says in his modesty to science, what God in his power says to the ocean: "Thus far shalt thou go, and no farther."

Doctor Chalmers was right; the limits of the finite world are those also of human science: how far within these vast limits science may extend her empire, who shall affirm? But what we certainly may assert is, that she never can exceed them. The finite world alone is within her reach, the only world that she can fathom. It is only in the finite world that man's mind can fully grasp the facts, observe them in all their extent, and under all their aspects, discriminate their relations and their laws (which constitute also a species of facts), and so verify the system to which they should be referred. This it is that makes what we term scientific processes and labour, and human sciences are the results.

What need to mention that in speaking of the finite world, I do not mean to speak of the material world alone? Moral facts there also are which fall under observation, and enter into the domain of science. The study of man in his actual condition, whether considered as an individual or as forming a member of a nation, is also a scientific study, subject to the same method as that of the material world: and it is its legitimate province also to detect in the actual order of this world the laws of those particular facts to which it addresses itself.

But if the limits of the finite world are those of human science, they are not those of the human soul. Man contains in himself ideas and ambitious aspirations extending far beyond and rising far above the finite world, ideas of and aspirations towards the Infinite, the Ideal, the Perfect, the Immutable, the Eternal. These ideas and aspirations are themselves realities admitted by the human mind; but even in admitting them man's mind comes to a halt; they give him a presentiment of, or to speak with more precision, a revelation of, an order of things different from the facts and laws of the finite world which lies under his observation; but whilst man has of this superior order the instinct and the perspective, he can have of it no positive knowledge. It proceeds from the sublimity of his nature if he has a glimpse of Infinity—if he aspires to it; whereas it results from the infirmity of his actual condition if his positive knowledge is limited by the world in which he exists.

I was born in the south, under the very sun. I have yet, for the most part, lived in regions either of the north, or bordering upon the north, regions so frequently immersed in mists. When under their pale sky we look towards the horizon, a fog of greater or less density limits the view; the vision itself might penetrate much farther, but an external obstacle arrests it; it does not find there the light it needs. Regard now the horizon under the pure and brilliant sky of the south; the plains, distant as well as near, are bathed in light; the human eye can penetrate there as far as its organization permits. If it pierces no farther, it is not for want of light, but because its proper and natural force has attained its limit: the mind knows that there are spaces beyond that which the eye traverses, but the eye penetrates them not. This is an image of what happens to the mind itself when contemplating and studying the universe: it reaches a point where its clear sight, that is to say its positive appreciation, halts, not that it finds there the end of things themselves, but the limit of man's scientific appreciation of them; other realities present themselves to him; he has a glimpse of them; he believes in them spontaneously and naturally; it is not given to him to grasp them and to measure them; but he can neither ignore them, nor know them, neither have positive knowledge of them, nor refrain from having faith in them.

I cannot deny myself the pleasure of citing what I wrote thirteen years ago upon the same subject, when philosophically examining the real meaning of the word ***faith***. "The object of every religious belief," said I, "is in a certain, a large measure, inaccessible to human science. Human science may establish that object's reality; it may arrive at the boundary of this mysterious world; and assure itself of the existence there of facts with which man's destiny is connected; but it is not given to it so to attain the facts themselves as to subject them to its examination.

"Their incapacity to do so has struck more than one philosopher, and has led them to the conclusion that no such reality exists, that every religious belief contemplates subjects simply chimerical. Others, shutting their eyes to their own incompetency, have dashed daringly forwards towards the sphere of the supernatural; and just as if they had succeeded in penetrating into it, they have described its facts, resolved its problems, assigned its laws. It is difficult to say who shows more foolish arrogance, the man who maintains that that of which he cannot have positive knowledge has no real existence, or the man who pretends to be able to know everything that actually exists. However this may be, mankind has never for a single day assented to either assertion: man's instincts and his actions have constantly disavowed both the negation of the disbeliever and the confidence of the theologian. In spite of the former, he has persisted in believing in the existence of the unknown world, and in the reality of the relations which connect him with it: and notwithstanding the powerful influences of the latter, he has refused to admit their having attained their object—raised the veil; and so man has continued to agitate the same problems, to pursue the same truths, as ardently and as laboriously as at the first day, just as if nothing had been done at all." [Footnote 23]

[Footnote 23: Meditations et Études Morales, p. 170. Paris, 1851.]

I have just read again the excellent compendium given by M. Cousin in his ***General History of Philosophy from the most Ancient Times to the End of the Eighteenth Century***. He establishes that all the philosophical labours of the human understanding have terminated in four great systems—sensualism, idealism, scepticism, and mysticism—the sole actors in that intellectual arena where, in all ages and amongst all nations, they are in turn in the position of combatants and of sovereigns. And, after having clearly characterised in their origin and their development these four systems, M. Cousin adds, "As for their intrinsic merits, habituate yourselves to this principle: they have existed; therefore they had their reason to exist; therefore they are true at least in part. Error is the law of our nature: to it we are condemned; and in all our opinions and all our words there is always a large allowance to be made for error, and too often for absurdity. But absolute absurdity does not enter into the mind of man; it is the excellence of man's thought, that without some leaven of truth it admits nothing, and absolute error is impossible. The four systems which have just been rapidly laid before you have had each their existence; therefore they contain truth, still without being entirely true. Partially true, and partially false, these systems reappear at all the great epochs. Time cannot destroy any one of them, nor can it beget any new one, because time develops and perfects the human mind, though without changing its nature and its fundamental tendencies. Time does no more than multiply and vary almost infinitely the combinations of the four simple and elementary systems. Hence originate those countless systems which history collects and which it is its office to explain." [Footnote 24]

> [Footnote 24: Histoire Générale de la Philosophic depuis les temps les plus anciens jusqu'à la fin du XVIII Siècle, par M. Victor Cousin, pp. 4-31. 1863.]

M. Cousin excels in explaining these numberless philosophical combinations, and in tracing them all back to the four great systems which he has defined; but there is a fact still more important than the variety of these combinations, and which calls itself for explanation. Why did these four essential systems—sensualism, idealism, scepticism, and mysticism, appear from the most ancient times? why have they continued to reproduce themselves always and everywhere, with deductions more or less logical, with greater or less ability, but still fundamentally always and everywhere the same? Why, upon these supreme questions, did the human mind achieve at so early a period, what may be termed, it is true, but essays at a solution, but which essays in some sort have exhausted the mind rather than satisfied it? How is it that these different systems, invented with such promptitude, have never been able either to come to an accord, nor has any one been able to prevail decidedly against another and to cause itself to be received as the truth? Why has philosophy, or, to speak more precisely, why have metaphysics, remained essentially stationary; great at their birth, but destined not to grow: whereas the other sciences—those styled natural sciences—have been essentially progressive: at first feeble, and making in succession conquest after conquest; these they have been able to retain, until they have formed a domain day by day more extended and less contested?

The very fact that suggests these questions contains the answer to them. Man has, upon the fundamental subject of metaphysics, a primitive light, rather the heritage and dowry of human nature, than the conquest of human science. The metaphysician appropriates it as a torch to lighten him on his obscure and ill-defined path. He finds in man himself a point of departure at once profound and certain; but his aim is God; that is to say, an aim above his reach.

Must we, then, renounce the study of the great questions which form the subject of metaphysics as a vain labour, where the human mind is turning indefinitely in the same circle, incapable not only of attaining the object which it is pursuing, but of making any advance in its pursuit?

Often, and with more ability than has been evinced by the Positive school of the present day, has this judgment been pronounced against metaphysics. But that judgment man's mind has never accepted, and never will accept; the great problems which pass beyond the finite world lie propounded before him;

never will he renounce the attempt to solve them; he is impelled to it by an irresistible instinct, an instinct full of faith and of hope, in spite of the repeated failure of his efforts. As man is in the sphere of action, so is he also in that of thought; he aspires higher than it is possible to achieve: this is his nature and his glory; to renounce his aspirations would be declaring his own forfeiture. But without any such abdication, it is still necessary that he should know himself, it is necessary that he should understand that his strength here below is infinitely less than his ambition, and that it is not given him to have any positive scientific knowledge of that infinite and ideal world towards which he dashes. The facts and the problems which he there encounters are such, that the methods and the laws which direct the human mind in the study of the finite world are inapplicable. The infinite is for us the object not of science but belief, and it is alike impossible for us either to reject or penetrate it. Let man, then, feel a profound sentiment of that double truth: let him, without sacrificing the ambitious aspirations of his intelligence, recognise the limits imposed upon his achievements in science; he will not then be long in also recognising that, in the relations of the finite with the infinite—of himself with God—he stands in need of superhuman assistance, and that this does not fail him. God has given to man what man never can conquer, and revelation opens to him that world of the infinite over which, by its own exertions and of itself alone, man's mind never could spread light. The light man receives from God himself.

Fifth Meditation.
Revelation.

When it was objected to Leibnitz "that there is nothing in the intelligence that has not first been in the sense," Leibnitz replied, "if not the intelligence itself." [Footnote 25]

> [Footnote 25: Nihil est in intellectu quod non prius fuerit in sensu.—Nisi intellectus ipse.]

In the answer of Leibnitz I will change but a single word, and substitute for ***intelligence, soul***. ***Soul*** is a term more comprehensive and more complete than ***intelligence;*** it embraces everything in the human being that is not body and matter; it is not the mere intelligence, a special faculty of man; it is all the intellectual and moral man.

The soul possesses itself and carries with it into life native faculties and an inborn light: these manifest and develop themselves more and more as they come into relation with the exterior world; but they had still an existence prior to those relations, and they exercise an important influence upon what results. The external world does not create nor essentially change the intellectual and moral being that has just come into life, but it opens to it a stage where that being acts in accordance at once with its proper nature, and the conditions and influences in the midst of which the action takes place. The hypothesis of a statue endowed with sensibility is a contradiction; in seeking to explain man's first growth, it loses sight of the entire intellectual and moral being.

When, as I said before, man first entered the world, he did not enter it, he could not enter it, as a new-born babe, with the mere breath of life; he was created full grown, with instincts and faculties complete in their power and capable of immediate action. We must either deny the creation and be driven to monstrous hypotheses, or admit that the human being who now develops himself slowly and laboriously, was at his first appearance mature in body and in mind.

The creation implies then the Revelation, a revelation which lighted man at his entrance into the world, and qualified him from that very moment to use his faculties and his instincts. Do we, can we, picture to ourselves the first man, the first human couple, with a complete physical development, and yet without the essential conditions of intellectual activity, physically strong and morally a nonentity, the body of twenty years and the soul in the first hour of infancy? Such a fact is self-contradictory, and impossible of conception.

What was the positive extent of this primal revelation, the necessary attendant upon creation, which occurred in the first relation of God with man? No man can say. I open the book of Genesis and there I read:

"And the Lord God took the man, and put him into the garden of Eden to dress it and to keep it. And the Lord God commanded the man, saying, Of every tree of the garden thou mayest freely eat: But of the tree of the knowledge of good and evil, thou shalt not eat of it: for in the day that thou eatest thereof thou shalt surely die. And the Lord God said, It is not good that the man should be alone; I will make him an help meet for him. And out of the ground the Lord God formed every beast of the field, and every fowl of the air; and brought them unto Adam to see what he would call them: and whatsoever Adam called every living creature, that was the name thereof. And Adam gave names to all cattle, and to the fowl of the air, and to every beast of the field; but for Adam there was not found an help meet for him. And the Lord God caused a deep sleep to fall upon Adam, and he slept: and he took one of his ribs, and closed up the flesh instead thereof; and the rib, which the Lord God had taken from man, made he a woman, and brought her unto the man. And Adam said, This is now bone of my bones, and flesh of my flesh. ... Therefore shall a man leave his father and his mother, and shall cleave unto his wife: and they shall be one flesh." [Footnote 26]

[Footnote 26: Genesis ii. 15-24.]

According, then, to the Bible, the primitive revelation essentially bore upon the three points,—marriage, language, and the duty of man's obedience to God his Creator: Adam received at the hand of God the moral law of his liberty, the companion of his life, and the faculty by which he was enabled to name the creatures that were around him: in other words, the three sources of religion, of family, and of science were immediately unclosed to him. It is not necessary here to enter upon any of the questions which have been raised, as to the human origin of language, the primitive language, or the formation of families, with their influence upon the great organisation of society: the limits of the primitive revelation cannot be determined scientifically; the fact of the revelation itself is certain. This is the light which lighted the first man from his first entrance upon life, and without which it is impossible to conceive that he could have survived.

The primitive revelation did not abandon mankind on its development and dispersion; it accompanied it everywhere, as a general and permanent revelation. The light which had lighted the first man spread amongst all nations and throughout all ages, assuming the character of ideas, universal and uncontested; of instincts, spontaneous and indestructible. No nation has been without this light, none left to its own unassisted efforts to grope its way through the darkness of life. Let not the human understanding pride itself too much upon its works; the glory does not belong to it alone: what it has accomplished it has accomplished by aid of the primitive principles received from God; in all his works and all his progress man has had for point of departure and support that primitive revelation. All the grand doctrines, all the mighty institutions, which have governed the world, whatever intermixture of monstrous and fatal errors they may have contained, have preserved a trace of the fundamental verities which were the dowry of humanity at its birth. God has forsaken no portion of the human race; and not less amidst the errors into which it has fallen, than in the noble developments which constitute its glory, we recognise signs of the primitive teaching derived from its Divine Author.

After the revelation made to the first man, and in the midst of the general revelation diffused over all mankind, a great event occurs in history: a special revelation takes place, and has for its seat the bosom of an inconsiderable nation, that had been shut in during sixteen centuries in a little corner of the world; and it was thence that, nineteen centuries ago, that revelation proceeded to enlighten and to subdue, according to the predictions of its Author, all the human race.

A man of an imagination as fertile as his knowledge is profound, who, with an admirable candour has in his works associated hypothesis and faith, M. Ewald, professor at the University of Göttingen, has recently thus characterised this event:—"The history of the old Jewish people is fundamentally the history of the true religion, proceeding from step to step to its complete development, rising through all kinds of struggles, until it achieves a supreme victory, and finally manifesting itself in all its majesty and power, in order to spread irresistibly, by its proper virtue, so as to become the eternal possession and blessing of all nations." [Footnote 27]

[Footnote 27: H. Ewald, Geschichte des Volkes Israel, bis Christus. 2nd ed., vol. i. p. 9. Göttingen, 1851.]

How is the great event thus characterised by M. Ewald proved? By what marks can we distinguish the Divine origin of this special revelation that became the Christian religion? What does it affirm itself in support of its claim to the moral conquest of mankind?

At the very outset, in proving her dogmas and precepts to have come from God, the Christian revelation asserts that the documents in which it is written are themselves of divine origin. The divine inspiration of the sacred volume is the first basis of the Christian Faith, the external title of Christianity to authority over souls. What is the full import of this title? What the signification of the inspiration of the sacred volumes?

Sixth Meditation.
The Inspiration Of The Scriptures.

I have read the sacred volumes over and over again, I have perused them in very different dispositions of mind, at one time studying them as great historical documents, at another admiring them as sublime works of poetry. I have experienced an extraordinary impression, quite different from either curiosity or admiration. I have felt myself the listener of a language other than that of the chronicler or the poet; and under the influence of a breath issuing from other sources than human. Not that man does not occupy a great place in the sacred volumes; he displays himself there, on the contrary, with all his passions, his vices, his weaknesses, his ignorance, his errors; the Hebrew people shows itself rude, barbarous, changeable, superstitious, accessible to all the imperfections, to all the failings, of other nations. But the Hebrew is not the sole actor in his history; he has an Ally, a Protector, a Master, who intervenes incessantly to command, inspire, direct, strike, or save. God is there, always present, acting—

> "Et ce n'est pas un Dieu comme vos dieux frivoles, Insensibles et sourds, impuissants, mutilés, De bois, de marbre, ou d'or, comme vous le voulez." [Footnote 28]
>
> "Not such a god as are ***your*** friv'lous gods, Insensible and deaf, weak, mutilated, Of wood, or stone, or gold, as ***you*** will have them."

[Footnote 28: Corneille, Polyeucte, acte iv. sc. 3.]

It is the God One and Supreme, All Powerful, the Creator, the Eternal. And even in their forgetfulness and their disobedience, the Hebrews believe still in God: He is still the object at once of their fear, of their hope, and of a faith that persists in the midst of the infidelity of their lives. The Bible is no poem in which man recounts and sings the adventures of his God combined with his own; it is a real drama, a continued dialogue between God and man personified in the Hebrews; it is, on the one side, God's will and God's action, and, on the other, man's liberty and man's faith, now in pious association, now at fatal variance.

The more I have perused the Scriptures, the more surprised I feel that earnest readers should not have been impressed as I have been, and that several should have failed to see the characteristic of divine inspiration, so foreign to every other book, so remarkable in this one. That men who absolutely deny all supernatural action of God in the world, should not be more disposed to admit it in the sources of the Bible than elsewhere, is perfectly comprehensible; but the attack upon the divine inspiration of the sacred books has another motive, and one more likely to prove contagious. It is not without deep regret that I proceed in this place to contradict ancient traditions, at once respected and respectable, and perhaps to offend sober and sincere convictions. But my own conviction is stronger than my regret, and it is still more so because accompanied by another conviction, which is, that the system that it is my intention to contest, has occasioned, continues to occasion, and may still occasion, an immense ill to Christianity.

Whoever reads without prejudice in the Hebrew and Greek the original texts of the Scriptures, whether of the Old or New Testament, meets there often in the midst of their sublime beauties, I do not say merely faults of style, but of grammar, in violation of those logical and natural rules of language common to all tongues. Are we to infer that these faults have the same origin as the doctrines with which they are intermixed, and that they are both divinely inspired? [Footnote 29]

> [Footnote 29: I indicate, in a note placed at the end of this volume, some instances of these grammatical faults met with in the Scriptures, and to which it is impossible to assign the character of divine inspiration.]

And yet this is what is pretended by fervent and learned men, who maintain that all, absolutely all, in the Scriptures is divinely inspired—the words as well as the ideas, all the words used upon all subjects, the material of language as well as the doctrine which lies at its base.

In this assertion I see but deplorable confusion, leading to profound misapprehension both of the meaning and the object of the sacred books. It was not God's purpose to give instruction to men in grammar, and if not in grammar, neither was it, any more God's purpose to give instruction in geology, astronomy, geography, or chronology. It is on their relations with their Creator, upon duties of men towards Him and towards each other, upon the rule of faith and of conduct in life, that God has lighted them by light from heaven. It is to the subject of religion and morals, and to these alone, that the inspiration of the Scriptures is directed.

Amongst the principal arguments alleged to prove that everything in the sacred volumes is divinely inspired, particular use has been made of the Second Epistle of St. Paul to Timothy, where in effect we find the passage:—

"All Scripture is given by inspiration of God, and is profitable for doctrine, for reproof, for correction, for instruction in righteousness:

"That the man of God may be perfect, thoroughly furnished unto all good works." [Footnote 30]

[Footnote 30: 2 Timothy iii. 16, 17.]

Is it possible to determine in words of greater precision the religious and moral object of the inspiration?

Appeal is made to a consideration of a different description. If, it is said, we at the same time admit, on the one side, the inspiration of the sacred books, and on the other, that this inspiration is not universal and absolute, who shall make the selection between these two parts?—who mark the limit of the inspiration?—who say which texts, which passages are inspired, and which are not? So to divide the Holy Scriptures is to strip them of their supernatural character, to destroy their authenticity, by surrendering them to all the incertitudes, all the disputes of men: a complete and uninterrupted inspiration alone is capable of commanding faith.

Never-dying pretension of man's weakness! Created intelligent and free, he proposes to use largely his intelligence and his freedom; at the same time, conscious how feeble his means are, how inadequate to his aspirations, he invokes a guide, a support; and from the very moment that his hope fixes upon it, he will have it immutable, infallible. He searches a fixed point to which to attach himself with absolute and permanent assurance. In creating man, God did not leave him without fixed points; the Divine revelation, and the inspiration of the Scriptures, had precisely for object and effect to supply these, but not on all subjects alike and without distinction. I refer here again to what I lately said respecting the separation of the finite and the infinite, of the world created, and of its Creator. At the same time that the limits of the finite world are those of human science, it is to human study and human science that God has surrendered the finite world; it is not there that God has set up his divine torch; He has dictated to Moses the laws which regulate the duties of man towards God, and of man towards man; but He has left to Newton the discovery of the laws which preside over the universe. The Scriptures speak upon all subjects; circumstances connected with the finite world are there incessantly mixed with perspectives of infinity; but it is only to the latter, to that future of which they permit us to snatch a view, and to the laws which they impose upon men, that the divine inspiration addresses itself; God only pours his light in quarters which man's eye and man's labour cannot reach; for all that remains, the sacred books speak the language used and understood by the generations to whom they are addressed. God does not, even when He inspires them, transport into future domains of science the interpreters He uses, or the nations to whom He sends them; He takes them both as He finds them, with their traditions, their notions, their degree of knowledge or ignorance as respects the finite world, of its phenomena and its laws. It is not the condition, the scientific progress of the human understanding; it is the condition and moral progress of the human soul which are the object of the Divine action, and God requires not for the exercise of his power on the human soul, science either as a precursor or a companion; He addresses himself to instincts and desires the most intimate and most sublime as well as the most universal in man's nature, to instincts and desires of which science is neither the object nor the measure, and which require to be satisfied from other sources. Whatever true or false science we find in the Scriptures upon the subject of the finite world, proceeds from the writers themselves or their contemporaries; they have spoken as they believed, or as those believed who surrounded them when they spoke: on the other hand, the light thrown over the infinite, the law laid down, and the perspective opened by that same light, these are what proceed from God, and which He has inspired in the Scriptures. Their object is essentially and exclusively moral and practical; they express the ideas, employ the images, and speak the language best calculated to produce a powerful effect upon the soul, to regenerate and to save it. I open the Gospel according to St. Luke, and I there read the admirable parable:—

> "There was a certain rich man, which was clothed in purple and fine linen, and fared sumptuously every day:
>
> "And there was a certain beggar named Lazarus, which was laid at his gate, full of sores,
>
> "And desiring to be fed with the crumbs which fell from the rich man's table: moreover the dogs came and licked his sores.
>
> "And it came to pass, that the beggar died, and was carried by the angels into Abraham's bosom: the rich man also died, and was buried;
>
> "And in hell he lift up his eyes, being in torments, and seeth Abraham afar off, and Lazarus in his bosom.
>
> "And he cried and said, Father Abraham, have mercy on me, and

send Lazarus, that he may dip the tip of his finger in water, and cool my tongue; for I am tormented in this flame.

"But Abraham said, Son, remember that thou in thy lifetime receivedst thy good things, and likewise Lazarus evil things; but now he is comforted, and thou art tormented.

"And beside all this, between us and you there is a great gulf fixed: so that they which would pass from hence to you cannot; neither can they pass to us, that would come from thence.

"Then he said, I pray thee therefore, father, that thou wouldest send him to my father's house:

"For I have five brethren; that he may testify unto them, lest they also come into this place of torment.

"Abraham saith unto him, They have Moses and the prophets; let them hear them.

"And he said, Nay, father Abraham: but if one went unto them from the dead, they will repent.

"And he said unto him, If they hear not Moses and the prophets, neither will they be persuaded, though one rose from the dead." [Footnote 31]

[Footnote 31: Luke xvi. 19-31.]

Was it the intention of Jesus, and of the Evangelist who has repeated his words, to describe, as they really are, the condition of men after their earthly existence, their positive local position after God's judgment, and their relations either with each other or with the world which they have quitted? Certainly not; the material circumstances intermixed with this dialogue are only images borrowed from actual common life. But what images so strike, so penetrate the soul? What more solemn warning addressed to men in this life, to rouse them to a sense of their duties towards God and their fellow creatures, in the name of the mysterious future that awaits them?

Nothing is further from my thought than to see in the sacred books mere poetical images and symbols; those books are really, with respect to the religious problems that beset man's thoughts, the Light and the voice of God; still, that Light only lights, that voice only reveals revelations of God with man, duties which God enjoins men in the course of their present life, and prospects which He opens to them beyond the imperfect and limited world where this life passes. As for this life itself, it is the object of human study and science, not of the inspiration of the sacred Scriptures. In disregarding this limit, in pretending to attribute to the language of the Scriptures, used with reference to the phenomena of the finite world, the character of divine inspiration, men have fallen with respect both to thought and act into deplorable errors. Hence proceeded the trial of Galileo, and numerous other controversies, numerous other condemnations still more absurd, still more to be regretted, in which Christianity was immediately placed in opposition to human science, and constrained to inflict or receive remarkable disavowals. The same is the case at the present day with respect to numerous objections made in the name of the natural sciences to Christianity, and which from the learned circles where they have their birth, spread over a world at once curious and frivolous, where they cause the Christian faith itself to be regarded as ignorant credulity. Nothing of this kind could ever occur, no necessity of such conflict could await the Christian religion, if on the one side the limits of human science, and on the other those of divine inspiration, were recognised as they really are, and respected according to their rightful claims.

I might cite in aid of the opinion I support numerous and great authorities. I will refer to but thrcc, appealed to by Galileo himself in 1615 in his letters to the Grand Duchess Christina of Lorraine" [Footnote 32]—(who could appeal to authorities more august?)—"Many things," says St. Jerome, "are recounted in the Scriptures according to the judgment of the times when they happened, and not according to the truth." [Footnote 33]

> [Footnote 32: Opere Complete di Galileo-Galilei, t. ii. chap. ii. pp. 26-64. Florence, 1843.]
>
> [Footnote 33: OEuvres de St. Jérôme, Comment, in Jeremiam, ed. Vallars. t. ix. p. 1040.]

> "The purpose of the Holy Scriptures," says the Cardinal Baronius, "is to teach us how to go to heaven, and not how the heavens go." "This," says Kepler, "is the counsel I give to the man so ill informed as not to understand the science of astronomy, or so weak as to regard adhesion to Copernicus as proof of want of piety:—Let him at once leave the study of astronomy and the examination of the opinions of philosophers; instead of devoting himself to those arduous researches, let him remain at home, till his fields, and occupy himself with his proper business; and thence, raising towards the admirable

vault of heaven his eyes, which constitute for him his sole mode of vision, let him pour forth his heart in thanksgivings and praises to God his Creator. He may rest assured that he is thus rendering to God a worship as perfect as that of the astronomer himself, to whom God has accorded the gift of seeing clearer with the eyes of his intelligence; but who, above all the worlds and all the heavens that he attains, knows and wills to find his God." [Footnote 34]

[Footnote 34: Kepler, Nova Astronomia, Introductio, p. 9. Prague, 1609.]

I discard, then, as absolutely foreign to the grand question that occupies me, all the difficulties suggested to the Scriptures in the name of those sciences whose province is finite nature. I seek and consider in these books only what is their sole object,—the relations of God with man, and the solution of those problems which these relations cause to weigh upon the human soul. The deeper we go in the study of the sacred volumes, restored to their real object, the more the divine inspiration becomes manifest and striking. God and man are there ever both present, both actors in the same history. Of this history it is my present object to illustrate the grand features.

Seventh Meditation.
God According To The Bible.

It is far from my intention to evade the questions which concern the authenticity of the Bible, and of the respective books which compose it. I shall enter upon them in the second series of these ***Meditations***, when I touch upon the history of the Christian religion. Those questions, however, have no bearing upon the subject which occupies me at the present moment; the Bible, whatever its antiquity, whatever the comparative antiquity of its different parts, has been ever that witness of God in which the Hebrews believed, and under the law of which they lived, the great monument of the religion in the bosom of which the Christian religion took its birth. It is this God of whom in the Bible, and in the Bible alone, it is my purpose to seek the peculiar and true character.

The nations of Semitic origin have been honoured for their primitive and persistent faith in the unity of God. Under different forms, and amidst events very dissimilar, nearly all nations have been polytheistic; the Semitic nations alone have believed firmly in the one God. This great moral fact has been attributed to different and to complex causes; but the fact itself is generally acknowledged and admitted.

In two respects in this assertion there is exaggeration. On one side, among the nations of Semitic origin, several were polytheistic; the descendants of Abraham, the Hebrews, and the Arab Ishmaelites, alone remained really monotheistic; on the other side, the idea of the unity of God was not entirely strange even to the polytheistic nations. The greater part, like the Hindoos and the Greeks, admitted one sole and primordial Power anterior and superior to their gods;—idea, vague and searched from afar, derived from the instinct of man or the reflection of the philosopher, and which amongst those nations became neither the basis of any religion that deserves the name, nor any efficacious obstacle to idolatry. The God of the Bible is no such sterile abstraction; He is the one God at the present time as in the origin of all things, the personal God, living, acting, and presiding efficiently over the destinies of the world that He has created.

He has besides another characteristic, one far more striking, which belongs to Him more exclusively than that of Unity. The gods of the polytheistic nations have histories filled with events, vicissitudes, transformations, adventures. The mythology of the Egyptians, of the Hindoos, of the Greeks, of the Scandinavians, and numerous others, is but the poetical or symbolical recital of the varied and agitated lives of their gods. We detect in these recitals sometimes the personification of the fancies of nations described in accordance with their actual phenomena, some times the reminiscences of human personages who have struck the imagination of the people. But whatever their origin, whatever their name, each of those gods has his individual history more or less overladen with incidents and acts, now heroic, now licentious, now elegantly fantastic, now grossly eccentric. All the polytheistic religions are collections of biographies, divine or legendary, allegorical or completely fabulous, in which the careers and the passions, the actions and the dreams of men, reproduce themselves under the forms and names of deities.

The God of the Bible has no biography, neither has He any personal adventures. Nothing occurs to Him and nothing changes in Him; He is always and invariably the same, a Being real and personal, absolutely distinct from the finite world and from humanity, identical and immutable in the bosom of the universal diversity and movement. "I Am That I Am," is the sole definition that He vouchsafes of himself, and the constant expression of what He is in all the course of the history of the Hebrews, to which He is present and over which He presides without ever receiving from it any reflex of influence. Such is the God of the Bible, in evident and permanent contrast with all the gods of polytheism, still more distinct and more solitary by his nature than by his Unity.

This is, indeed, so peculiarly the proper and essential character of the God of the Bible, that this character has passed into the very language of the Hebrews, and has become there the very name of God. Several words are employed in the Bible as appellations of God. One of these ***El, Eloah,*** in the plural ***Elohïm***, expresses force, ***creative power***, and is applied to the manifold gods of Paganism as well as to the one God of the Hebrews. ***El Shaddaï*** is translated by ***the all-powerful***. ***Adonai*** signifies ***Lord***. The word ***Yahwe*** or ***Yehwe***, which becomes in Hebrew pronunciation ***Jehovah***, means simply ***He is***, and means self-existence, the Being Absolute and Eternal. This name occurs in no other of the Semitic languages, and it is at the epoch of Moses that it appears for the first time amongst the Hebrews: "And God spake unto Moses, and said unto him, I am the Eternal" (***Yahwe, Jehovah***). "And I appeared unto Abraham, Isaac, and unto Jacob, by the name of the All-powerful (***El Shaddaï***), but by my name Eternal was I not known to them." [Footnote 35] ***Yahwe, Jehovah***, is at once the true God and the national God of Israel. [Footnote 36]

[Footnote 35: Exodus vi. 2, 3.]

[Footnote 36: I have consulted respecting the precise

sense and the different shades of meaning of the terms expressing God in Hebrew, my learned ***confrère*** at the Academy of Inscriptions, M. Munk, who has replied to all my inquiries with as much clearness as courtesy.]

The history of the Hebrews is neither less significant nor less expressive than their language; it is the history of the relations of the God, One and Immutable with the people chosen by Him to be the special representative of the religious principle, and the regenerating source of religious life in the human race. This people undergoes the destiny and trials common to all nations; it demands, and becomes subject to, a variety of different governments; it falls into the errors and faults usual to nations; it frequently succumbs to the temptations of idolatry; like the others, it has its days of virtue and of vice, of prosperity and of reverses, of glory and of abasement. Amidst all the vicissitudes and errors of the people of the Bible, the God of the Bible remains invariably the same, without any tincture of anthropomorphism, without any alteration in the idea which the Hebrews conceive of his nature, either during their fidelity or disobedience to his Commandments. It is always the God who has said, "I Am That I Am," of whom his people demand no other explanation of himself, and who, ever present and sovereign, pursues the designs of his providence with men, who either use or abuse the liberty of action which that God had accorded to them at their creation. I wish to retrace, according to the Bible, the principal phases and the principal actors in this history. The more I study, the more I feel that I am watching, as M. Ewald has expressed it, "the career of the true religion, advancing step by step to its complete development," that is to say, that I am there observing the action of God upon the first steps and upon the religious progress of the human race.

I. God And Abraham.

The history of the Hebrews, temporal and spiritual, opens with Abraham. At his first appearance in the Bible, Abraham is a nomad chief, who has quitted Chaldæa and the town of Haran, where his father, Terah, descended from Shem, is still living. He is wandering with his family, his servants, and his flocks, at first on the frontiers and afterwards in the interior of the land of Canaan, halting wherever he finds water and pasturage, and conducting his tents and his tribe at one time through the mountainous districts, at another along the plains below. Why has he left Chaldæa? According to the Bible itself, his father was an idolater: "Your fathers," said Joshua to the people of

Israel, "dwelt on the other side of the flood" (the Euphrates) "in old time, even Terah, the father of Abraham, and the father of Nachor: and they served other gods." [Footnote 37] The book of Judith contains a similar assertion; [Footnote 38] and the Jewish and Arabian traditions confirm, at the same time that they amplify, the statement: the father of Abraham, they say, was an idolatrous fanatic, and his son Abraham, having set himself against the practice of idolatry, was upon his charge thrown into a burning furnace, from which a miracle alone preserved him. The historian Josephus speaks of the insurrections which took place amongst the Chaldæans on the occasion of their religious dissensions.

[Footnote 37: Joshua xxiv. 2.]

[Footnote 38: Judith v. 6-9.]

[USCCB: Judith v. 6-9. "These people are descendants of the Chaldeans. They formerly dwelt in Mesopotamia, for they did not wish to follow the gods of their forefathers who were born in the land of the Chaldeans. Since they abandoned the way of their ancestors, and acknowledged with divine worship the God of heaven, their forefathers expelled them from the presence of their gods. So they fled to Mesopotamia and dwelt there a long time. Their God bade them leave their abode and proceed to the land of Canaan. Here they settled, and grew very rich in gold, silver, and a great abundance of livestock."]

The Bible makes no allusion to these traditions; from the very beginning God intervenes in the history of the father of the Hebrews. "The Eternal had said unto Abram, Get thee out of thy country, and from thy kindred, and from thy father's house, unto a land that I will shew thee: I will make thee a great nation, and I will bless thee, and make thy name great; ... and in thee shall all families of the earth be blessed. ... So Abram departed, ... and Abram took Sarai his wife, and Lot his brother's son, and all their substance that they had gathered, and the sons that they had gotten in Haran; and they went forth to go into the land of Canaan; and into the land of Canaan they came." [Footnote 39]

[Footnote 39: Genesis xii. 1-5.]

How had God spoken to Abraham? By a voice from without or by an internal inspiration? The writer of the Biblical narrative occupies himself in no respect with the question. God is for him, present and an actor in the history just as much as Abraham is; the intervention of God has in his eyes nothing but what is perfectly simple and natural. The same faith animates Abraham; he issues forth from Chaldæa and wanders through Palestine, according to the word and under the direction of the Eternal.

He wanders through the midst of populations already established upon the land of Canaan, and with these he lives in peace, but still, not uniting with them; bringing them succour when attacked by foreign chieftains; fighting in their behalf as a faithful ally, sometimes, perhaps, in the character of a valiant ***condottiere*** [mercenary], but remaining isolated in his capacity of nomad Patriarch, with his family and his tribe; repelling even the gifts and favours which might perhaps lower his character or affect his independence. Everywhere that he halts, or that any incident of importance occurs to him, at Sichem, Bethel, Beersheba, Hebron, he raises an altar to his God. In his wandering uncertain life a famine impels him on one occasion even as far as Egypt:—the first perhaps of those shepherd chiefs who issued from Asia, and who were so soon to invade that rich country. Abraham passes in Egypt several years, well treated by the reigning Pharaoh; on excellent terms with the Egyptian priests, imparting to them and receiving from them such knowledge of astronomy or of natural philosophy as they mutually possessed; but maintaining ever carefully the isolation of his family, of his tribe, and of his religion. Of his own accord, or at the instance of the Pharaoh, he quits Egypt, carrying with him not only his flocks and his camels, but his Egyptian slaves, and amongst others Hagar. He returns to the country of Canaan, again wanders through several of its districts, takes part in different events—internal troubles or foreign wars, and finally settles with his family and dependents at Hebron, near the oaks of Mamre, amongst the tribe of the children of Heth; but still always in his capacity as a foreigner, and always careful as such to preserve his character and his independence. When his wife Sarah died, the book of Genesis tells us that,

> "Abraham stood up from before his dead, and spake unto the sons of Heth, saying,
>
> "I am a stranger and a sojourner with you: give me a possession of a buryingplace with you, that I may bury my dead out of my sight.
>
> "And the children of Heth answered Abraham, saying unto him,
>
> "Hear us, my lord: thou art a mighty prince among us: in the choice of our sepulchres bury thy dead; none of us shall withhold from thee his sepulchre, but that thou mayest bury thy dead.

"And Abraham stood up, and bowed himself to the people of the land, even to the children of Heth.

"And he communed with them, saying, If it be your mind that I should bury my dead out of my sight; hear me, and entreat for me to Ephron the son of Zohar,

"That he may give me the cave of Machpelah, which he hath, which is in the end of his field; for as much money as it is worth he shall give it me for a possession of a buryingplace amongst you.

"And Ephron dwelt among the children of Heth: and Ephron the Hittite answered Abraham in the audience of the children of Heth, even of all that went in at the gate of his city, saying,

"Nay, my lord, hear me: the field give I thee, and the cave that is therein, I give it thee; in the presence of the sons of my people give I it thee: bury thy dead.

"And Abraham bowed down himself before the people of the land.

"And he spake unto Ephron in the audience of the people of the land, saying, But if thou wilt give it, I pray thee, hear me: I will give thee money for the field; take it of me, and I will bury my dead there.

"And Ephron answered Abraham, saying unto him,

"My lord, hearken unto me: the land is worth four hundred shekels of silver; what is that betwixt me and thee? bury therefore thy dead.

"And Abraham hearkened unto Ephron; and Abraham weighed to Ephron the silver, which he had named in the audience of the sons of Heth, four hundred shekels of silver, current money with the merchant.

"And the field of Ephron, which was in Machpelah, which was before Mamre, the field, and the cave which was therein, and all the trees that were in the field, that were in all the borders round about, were made sure

"Unto Abraham for a possession in the presence of the children of Heth, before all that went in at the gate of his city.

"And after this, Abraham buried Sarah his wife in the cave of the field of Machpelah before Mamre: the same is Hebron in the land of Canaan.

"And the field, and the cave that is therein, were made sure unto Abraham for a possession of a buryingplace by the sons of Heth." [Footnote 40]

[Footnote 40: Genesis xxiii. 3-20.]

Little importance does Abraham attach to his precarious condition as a wanderer and a stranger; he has faith in God. God commands, and Abraham obeys. God promises, and Abraham trusts. One day, however, with a feeling of anxious humility, Abraham makes the following prayer to God:—

"Lord Eternal, what wilt thou give me, seeing I go childless, and there is Eliezer of Damascus shall be my heir? And behold the word of the Lord came unto him, saying, This shall not be thine heir, but he that shall come forth out of thine own bowels shall be thine heir. I am God, the mighty, all-powerful; walk before my face, be thou perfect. I will establish my covenant between me and thee, and thy seed after thee, in their generation, for an everlasting possession, and I will be their God. But thou shalt keep my covenant therefore, thou and thy seed after thee, in their generations. And Abraham believed in the Lord; and the Eternal counted it to him for righteousness." [Footnote 41]

[Footnote 41: Genesis xv. 1-6. and xvii. 1-9.]

In these days, in the bosom of Christian civilization, obedience to God and confidence in God are the first precepts, the first virtues of Christianity. They were also the virtues of Abraham, and the precepts inculcated by Abraham's history in the Bible. And the God of Abraham, the God of the Bible, is the same who is the object of adoration to the Christian of the present day; the same conception as that of those philosophers of the present day who believe in God, and believe in Him as in God Absolute and Perfect, Self-dependent, Eternal, without the possibility or attempt to define Him otherwise. Thousands of years have changed nothing as to the biblical notion of God in the human soul, nor as to the essential laws regulating the relation of man with God.

Historical tradition fully confirms the moral fact here mentioned. Abraham has not been the object of any mystical conception, or any mythological metamorphosis; nowhere has he been transformed into demigod or son of God; he has ever remained the model of religious faith and submission, the type of the pious man in intimate relation with God. Throughout all antiquity, and in all the East, as much for the primitive Christians as for the Jews and Arabs, as much for the Mussulmans as for the Jews and Christians, God is the God of Abraham; Abraham is the friend of God, the father and the prince of believers; these are the very names that the Gospel gives him; [Footnote 42] and the Koran, too, celebrates him in these words:—

> [Footnote 42: St. Paul's Epistle to the Romans iv.; Galatians iii.; Epistle of St. James ii. 23.]

> "And when the night overshadowed him, he saw a star, and he said, This is my Lord; but when it set, he said, I like not gods which set. And when he saw the moon rising, he said, This is my Lord; but when he saw it set, he said, Verily, if my Lord direct me not, I shall become one of the people who go astray. And when he saw the sun rising, he said, This is my Lord, this is the greatest; but when it set, he said, my people, verily I am clear of that which ye associate with God. I direct my face unto him who hath created the heavens and the earth." [Footnote 43]

> [Footnote 43: Koran vi.]

The Eternal, the God One and Immutable, is the God of Abraham; Abraham is the servant and adorer of the true God.

II. God And Moses.

The true idea of God, and the faith in his effectual and continued providence, are the two great religious principles which the name of Abraham suggests. This is the beginning of the history of the Hebrews, and the origin of that ancient Covenant which, in passing from the Pentateuch to the Gospel, has become the new Covenant, the Christian Religion.

About five centuries later, we find the Hebrews settled in Egypt, in the land of Goshen, between the lower Nile, the Red Sea, and the Desert, in a condition very different from that in which they had first been when attracted to the court of Pharaoh by the prosperity of Joseph, the great-grandson of Abraham. The new Pharaoh oppresses them cruelly; they are a prey to the miseries of slavery, the contagion of idolatry, to all the evils, all the perils, physical and moral, which can afflict a nation numerically weak, fallen under the yoke of one powerful and civilized. The Hebrews nevertheless persist in their religious faith, cling to their national reminiscences; they do not suffer their nationality to be lost in and confounded with that of their masters; they endure without offering any active resistance; they will not deliver themselves, but they have never ceased to believe in their God, and they await their Deliverer.

Moses has been saved from the waters of the Nile by Pharaoh's own daughter. He has been brought up at Heliopolis, in the midst of the pomp of the court, and instructed in the sciences of the Egyptian priests. He has served the sovereign of Egypt; he has commanded his troops and made war for him against the Æthiopians. He has received an Egyptian name, Osarsiph, or Tisithen. Everything seems to concur to make him an Egyptian. But he remains a faithful Israelite: true to the faith and to the fortunes of his brethren. Their oppression rouses his indignation; he avenges one of them by killing his oppressor. The victims of oppression, alarmed, disavow Moses, instead of supporting him. Moses flees from Egypt and takes refuge in the Desert, amongst a tribe of wandering Arabs, the Midianites, sprung, like himself, from Abraham. Their chief, the sheick of the tribe, Jethro, called also Hobab, receives him as a son, and gives him his daughter Zipporah in marriage. The proud Israelite, who has declined to remain an Egyptian, becomes an Arab, and leads, several years, the nomadic life of the hospitable tribe. It is now in the peninsula of Sinai that Moses wanders with the servants and flocks of his father-in-law. In the centre of that peninsula, of yore a province in the empire of the Pharaohs, but which had fallen into the possession of the pastoral Arabs, rises Sinai, a mount with which from time immemorial, among the neighbouring tribes, have been connected as many sacred traditions as have ever been assigned to Mount Ararat in Armenia, or the Himalayas in India. In this venerable spot, before a burning bush, Moses, with a heart full of faith, hears God calling him and commanding him to lead his people, the children of Israel, out of Egypt. Moses is humble, distrustful of himself, just as Abraham before him had been. "Who am I, that I should go unto Pharaoh, and that I should bring forth the children of Israel out of Egypt? ... When I come unto the children of Israel, and shall say unto them, The God of your fathers hath sent me unto you; and they shall say to me, What is his name? What shall I say unto them? And God said unto Moses I AM THAT I AM: and he said, Thus shalt thou say unto the children of Israel, I AM hath sent me unto you." [Footnote 44]

[Footnote 44: Exodus iii. 11, 13, 14.]

Moses receives his mission from Jehovah, and feels no other disquietude than arises from the desire to accomplish it.

In presence of such facts, with this association of God and man in the same work, the opponents of the Supernatural still clamour: "Why," ask they, "this confusion of divine action and of human action? Has God need of man's concurrence? Can He not, if He will, accomplish all his designs by himself, and through the fulness of his omnipotence?" In my turn, I would ask them if they know why God created man, and if God has put them into the secret of his intentions towards the instrument whom He employs for his designs? There precisely lies the privilege of humanity: man is God's associate, subject to Him, yet a free agent independent of Him; he intervenes by his proper action in plans of which only an infinitely small part is revealed to his intelligence and reserved for his execution. Western Asia and its history are full of the name of Moses: Jews, Christians, and Mahometans style him the First Prophet, the Great Lawgiver, the Great Theologian; everywhere, in the scene of the events themselves, the places retain a memory of him: the traveller meets there the Well of Moses, the Ravine of Moses, the Mountain of Moses, the Valley of Moses. In other countries and other ages, this name has been given as the most glorious that the saints could receive: St. Peter has been styled the Moses of the Christian Church; St. Benedict, the Moses of the Monastic Orders; Ulphilas, the Moses of the Goths. What did Moses do to obtain a renown so great and so enduring? He gained no battles; he conquered no territory; he founded no cities; he governed no state; he was not even a man in whom eloquence replaced other sources of influence and power: "And Moses said unto the Lord, my Lord, I am not eloquent, neither heretofore, nor since thou hast spoken unto thy servant: but I am slow of speech, and of a slow tongue." [Footnote 45]

[Footnote 45: Exodus iv. 10.]

There is not in this whole history a single grand human action, a single grand event, proceeding from human agency; all, all is the work of God; and Moses is nothing on any occasion but the interpreter and instrument of God: to this mission he has consecrated soul and life; it is only by virtue of this title that he is powerful, and that he shares, as far as his capacity as a man permits, a work infinitely grander and more enduring than that accomplished by all the heroes and all the masters that the world ever acknowledged.

I know no more striking spectacle than that of the unshakeable faith and inexhaustible energy of Moses in the pursuit of a work not his own, in which he executes what he has not conceived, in which he obeys rather than commands. Obstacles and disappointments meet him at each turn; he has to struggle with weaknesses, infidelity, caprices, jealousies, and seditions, and these not merely in his own nation, but in his own family. He has himself his moments of sadness, of disquietude: "And Moses cried unto the Lord, saying,

What shall I do unto this people? they be almost ready to stone me.... [Footnote 46] I beseech thee, shew me thy glory."

[Footnote 46: Exodus xvii. 4; xxxiii. 18-20.]

And God answers him, "I will make all my goodness pass before thee. ... Thou canst not see my face: for there shall no man see me, and live." And Moses trusts in God, and continues to triumph whilst he obeys Him.

The work of deliverance is consummated; Moses has led the people of Israel out of Egypt, has surmounted the first perils and the first sufferings of the Desert. They advance through the group of mountains in the peninsula of Sinai Passing from valley to valley, they arrive "at the entrance of a large basin surrounded by lofty peaks. Of these the one which commands the most extensive view is covered with enormous blocks, as if the mountain had been overthrown by an earthquake. A deep cleft divides the peak into two.

"No one who has approached the Râs Sufsâfeh through that noble plain, or who has looked down upon the plain from that majestic height, will willingly part with the belief that these are the two essential features of the view of the Israelitish camp. That such a plain should exist at all in front of such a cliff is so remarkable a coincidence with the sacred narrative, as to furnish a strong internal argument, not merely of its identity with the scene, but of the scene itself having been described by an eyewitness. The awful and lengthened approach, as to some natural sanctuary, would have been the fittest preparation for the coming scene. The low line of alluvial mounds at the foot of the cliff exactly answers to the 'bounds' which were to keep the people off from 'touching the Mount.' [Footnote 47]

[Footnote 47: Exodus xix. 12.]

The plain itself is not broken and uneven, and narrowly shut in, like almost all others in the range, but presenting a long retiring sweep, against which the people could remove and stand afar off.' The cliff, rising like a huge altar in front of the whole congregation, and visible against the sky in lonely grandeur from end to end of the whole plain, is the very image of the 'mount that might not be touched,' and from which 'the voice' of God might be heard far and wide over the stillness of the plain below, widened at that point to its utmost extent by the confluence of all the contiguous valleys. Here, beyond all other parts of the peninsula, is the adytum, withdrawn, as if in the end of the world,' from all the stir and confusion of earthly things." [Footnote 48] Such was three thousand five hundred years ago, and such is still, the place where Moses received from God and gave to the people of Israel that law of the Ten Commandments which resound still through all the Christian

Churches as the first foundation of their faith and the first moral rule of Christian nations.

[Footnote 48: Sinai and Palestine in connection with their History. By Arthur Stanley, Dean of Westminster, pp. 42, 43. London, 1862.]

The Hebrews, at the moment when the Decalogue became their fundamental law, were in a crisis of social transformation; they were upon the point of passing from the pastoral nomadic condition to that of farmers and settlers. It seems that, at such an epoch, the political institutions of a people would, as the basis of their government, be its most natural and most urgent business. The Decalogue leaves the subject entirely untouched; makes to it not the remotest, the most indirect allusion. It is a law exclusively religious and moral, which only busies itself about the duties of man to God and to his fellow-creatures, and admits by its very silence all the varying forms of government that the external or internal state of society may seem to require. Characteristic, grand, and original, not to be met with in the primitive laws of any other nascent state, and an admirable and remarkable manifestation of the Divine origin of this one! It is to man's natural and his moral destiny that the Decalogue addresses itself; it is to guide man's soul and his inmost will that it lays down rules; whereas it surrenders his external, his civil condition to all the varying chances of place and of time.

Another characteristic of this law is not less original or less urgent: it places God, and man's duties towards God, at the head and front of man's life and man's duties; it unites intimately religion and morality, and regards them as inseparable. If philosophers, in studying, discriminate between them; if they seek in human nature the special principle or principles of morality; if they consider the latter by itself and apart from religion, it is the right of science to do so. But still the result is but a scientific work—only a partial dissection of man's soul, addressed to only one part of its faculties, and holding no account of the entirety and the reality of the soul's life. The Human Body, taken as one whole, is by nature at once moral and religious; the moral law that he finds in himself needs an author and a judge; and God is to him the source and guarantee, the Alpha and Omega of morality.

A metaphysician may, from time to time, affirm the moral law, and yet forget its Divine Author. A man may, now and then, admit, may respect the principles of morality, and yet remain estranged from religion; all this is possible, for all this we see. So small a portion of Truth sometimes satisfies the human mind! Man is so ready and so prone to misconceive and to mutilate himself! His ideas are by nature so incomplete and inconsequent, so easily dimmed or perverted by his Passions or the action of his free will!

These are but the exceptional conditions of the human mind, mere scientific abstractions; if men admit them, their influence is neither general nor durable. In the natural and actual life of the human race, Morality and Religion are necessarily united; and it is one of the divine characteristics of the Decalogue, as it is also one of the causes of that authority which has remained to it after the lapse of so many centuries, that it has proclaimed and taken as its foundation their intimate union.

This is not the place to consider the laws of Moses in civil and penal matters, nor to refer to his ordinances respecting the worship, or to those that regard the organization of the priesthood of the Hebrews. In the former of these two branches of the Mosaic code, numerous dispositions, singularly moral, equitable, and humane, are found in connection with circumstances indicating a state of manners gross and cruel even to barbarism.

The legislator is evidently under the empire of ideas and sentiments infinitely superior to those of the people, to whom, nevertheless, his strong sympathies attach him. When we consider the Mosaic Legislation, we find that in everything which concerns the external forms and practices of worship, the ideas of Egypt have made great impression upon the mind of the Lawgiver, and the frequent use that he has made of Egyptian customs and ceremonies is not less visible. But far above these institutions and these traditions, which seem not seldom out of place and incoherent, soars and predominates constantly the Idea of the God of Abraham and of Jacob, of the God One and Eternal, of the True God. The Laws of Moses omit no occasion of inculcating the belief in that God, and of recalling Him to the recollection of the Hebrews. And this, not as if they were recalling a principle, an institution, a system; but as if they propose to place a sovereign, a lawful and living sovereign, in the presence of those whom he governs, and to whom they owe obedience and fidelity.

Moses never speaks in his own name, or in the name of any human power, or of any portion of the Hebrew nation. God alone speaks and commands. God's word and his commands Moses repeats to the people. At his first ascending Mount Sinai, when he had received the first inspiration from the Eternal, "Moses came and called for the elders of the people, and laid before their faces all these words which the Lord commanded him. And all the people answered together, and said, All that the Lord hath spoken we will do." [Footnote 49]

[Footnote 49: Exodus xix. 7, 8.]

When Moses, again ascending Mount Sinai, had received from God the Decalogue, he returned, "And he took the book of the covenant, and read in the audience of the people: and they said, All that the Lord hath said will we do, and be obedient." [Footnote 50]

[Footnote 50: Exodus xxiv. 7.]

As the events develop themselves, the Hebrews are found far from rendering a constant obedience: they forget, they infringe—and that frequently—these laws of God which they have accepted; and God sometimes punishes, sometimes pardons them; still it is always God alone that is acting; it is from Him alone that all emanates; neither the priests who preside over the ceremonies of his worship, nor the elders of Israel whom He summons to prostrate themselves from afar before Him, nor Moses himself—his sole and constant interpreter—do anything by themselves, demand anything for themselves. The Pentateuch is the history and the picture of the personal government by God of the Israelites. "Our legislator," says the historian Josephus, "had in his thoughts not monarchies, nor oligarchies, nor democracies, nor any one of those political institutions: he commanded that our government should be (if it is permitted to make use of an expression somewhat exaggerated) what may be styled a Theocracy." [Footnote 51]

[Footnote 51: Joseph. contra Apionem, ii. c. 17.]

The eminent writers who have recently studied most profoundly the Mosaic system—M. Ewald in Germany,[Footnote 52] Mr. Milman and Mr. Arthur Stanley in England, M. Nicolas in France—have adopted the expression of Josephus, attaching to it its real and complete sense. "The term Theocracy," says Mr. Stanley, "has been often employed since the time of Moses, but in the sense of a sacerdotal government: a sense the very contrary to that in which its first author conceived it. The theocracy of Moses was not at all a government by priests, or opposed to kings; it was the government by God himself, as opposed to a government by priests or by kings." [Footnote 53]

[Footnote 52: Geschichte des Volkes Israel, bis Christus, ii. 188. Göttingen, 1853.]

[Footnote 53: Lectures on the Jewish Church, p. 157]

"Mosaism," says M. Nicolas, "is a theocracy in the proper sense of the word. It would be a complete error to understand this word in the sense which usage has given to it in our language. There is no question here in effect of a government exercised by a sacerdotal caste in the name and under the inspiration, real or pretended, of God. In the Mosaic legislation the priests are not the ministers and instruments of the Divine Will; God reigns and governs by himself. It is He who has given his laws to the Hebrews. Moses has been, it is true, the medium between the Eternal and the people, but the people has taken part in the grand spectacle of the Revelation of the Law; of this the people, in the exercise of its freedom, has evinced its acceptance; and in the covenant set on foot between the Eternal and the family of Jacob, Moses has been, if I may be allowed the expression, only the public officer who has propounded the contract. He was himself, besides, not within the pale of the sacerdotal caste; and the charge of keeping, amending, and seeing to the carrying out of the body of laws was not confided to the priests." [Footnote 54]

> [Footnote 54: Études Critiques sur la Bible—Ancien Testament, p. 172.]

Let the learned men who thus characterise the Mosaic theocracy pause here and measure the whole bearing of the fact which they comprehend so well. It is a fact unique in the history of the world. The idea of God is, amongst all nations, the source of religions; but in every case, except that of the Hebrews, scarcely has the source appeared before it deviates and becomes troubled; men take the place of God; God's name is made to cover every kind of usurpation and falsehood; sometimes sacerdotal corporations take possession of all government, civil and religious; sometimes secular power overrules and enslaves Religious Faith and Religious Life. In the Mosaic Dispensation we have nothing of the kind; its very origin and its fundamental principles condemn and prohibit even the attempt at any such deviations. No paramount priesthood here; no secular power playing the part of the oppressor. God is constantly present, and sole Master. All passes between God and the people; all, I say, so passes through the agency of a single man whom God inspires, and in whom the people have faith, asking no other authority than that of the revelation which he receives. No sign here of a fact of human origin: just as the God of the Bible is the true God, the religion that descended, by Moses, from Sinai upon the elect people of God is the true Religion destined to become, when Jesus Christ ascends Calvary, the Religion of the Human Race.

III. God And The Kings.

Moses having brought out of Egypt the people of Israel, and having conducted it through the Desert as far as the eastern bank of the Jordan, in sight of Canaan, the Promised Land, his mission terminates. "Get thee up," says the Eternal to him; "get thee up into the top of Pisgah, and lift up thine eyes westward, and northward, and southward, and eastward, and behold it with thine eyes: for thou shalt not go over this Jordan. But charge Joshua, and encourage him, and strengthen him: for he shall go over before this people, and he shall cause them to inherit the land which thou shalt see." [Footnote 55]

[Footnote 55: Deuteronomy iii. 27, 28.]

Moses has been, in the name of Jehovah, the liberator and the legislator; Joshua is the conqueror, the rough warrior, of yet signal piety and modesty, the ardent servant of Jehovah, the faithful disciple of Moses. After passing the Jordan, traversing the land of Canaan in every direction, and giving battle in succession to the greater part of the tribes that inhabit it, he destroys, or expels, or negotiates with them, and divides their lands among the twelve tribes of Israel. These exchange their wandering life for that settled agricultural life of which Moses has given them the law. The descendants of Abraham settle as masters in the soil in which Abraham had demanded as a favour the privilege of purchasing a tomb.

The consequences of this new situation are not long in showing themselves. The conquest is protracted and difficult: the violence and rapine that characterise a state of war—one of dispossession and of extermination—replace amongst the Hebrews the adventures and the pious emotions of the Desert. In spite of their successes, the conquest nevertheless remains incomplete: several of the Canaanitish tribes defend themselves efficaciously, and cling, side by side with the new comers, to their territory, their laws, their gods. The twelve tribes of Israel disperse and settle, each on its own account, upon different and distant points, some being even separated by the Jordan. The unity of the Hebrew nation, of its faith, of its law, of its government, and of its destiny weakens rapidly; the tendency to idolatry, which the Hebrews had so often evinced when wandering in the Desert, reappears and developes itself, fomented by the vicinity of the Polytheistic tribes of Canaan. Not, however, that we can precisely say that Polytheism prevails against the One God; but rather that material images of Jehovah become, in the midst of particular tribes, the object of the idolatrous worship so strongly prohibited by the Decalogue. "And the children of Israel did evil in the sight of the Lord, and forgat the Lord their God, and served Baalim and the groves." [Footnote 56]

[Footnote 56: Judges iii. 7.]

Under such influences the moral and social state of the people of Israel undergoes profound changes; the barbarism, which had been formerly amongst them fanatical and austere, becomes unruly and licentious; their chiefs, their Judges, during the epoch which bears their name, no longer possess, sometimes no longer merit, their confidence; even the heroic acts of some amongst them—of Gideon, of Deborah, of Samson,—present rather a strange than an august character. The Mosaic Theocracy veils itself; the Hebrew nation becomes disorganized; day by day, the religious and political anarchy in Israel extends and becomes aggravated.

But where the Divine Light has once shone, it is never completely extinguished; and when the voice of God has once spoken, the sound is never entirely lost, even to ears that no longer listen. It has been affirmed that after Joshua, in the lapse of time that took place between the government of the Judges and the end of the reign of Solomon, the recollection of Moses, of his actions and his laws, had almost entirely disappeared—had lost all authority in Israel. Some passages from the biblical narrative will suffice to remove this error. I read in the Book of Judges, with respect to the Canaanitish tribes who resisted and survived in their countries the conquest and settlement of the Hebrew tribes:—These nations "were to prove Israel, to know whether they would hearken unto the commandments of the Lord, which he commanded their fathers by the hand of Moses." [Footnote 57]

[Footnote 57: Judges iii. 4.]

And again, in the Book of Samuel, it is the Eternal "that advanced Moses and Aaron .... which brought forth your fathers out of the land of Egypt, and made them dwell in this place." [Footnote 58] And in the Book of Kings,[Footnote 59] David, on the point of expiring, says to his son Solomon, "Keep the charge of the Lord thy God, to walk in his ways, to keep his statutes, and his commandments, and his judgments, and his testimonies, as it is written in the law of Moses."

[Footnote 58: 1 Samuel xii. 6, 8.]

[Footnote 59: 1 Kings ii. 3.]

And when Solomon, after the solemn dedication of his Temple, had addressed to God his prayer of thanksgiving, "he stood, and blessed all the congregation of Israel with a loud voice, saying, Blessed be the Lord, that hath given rest unto his people Israel, according to all that he promised: there hath not failed one word of all his good promise, which he promised by the hand of Moses his servant." [Footnote 60]

[Footnote 60: 1 Kings viii. 55, 56.]

In the customs and lives of the Israelites these "good promises" had not practically, it is true, preserved all their efficacy: the worship of Jehovah and the legislation of Moses had fallen into sad oblivion, and undergone serious changes. But, in the national sentiment, Jehovah the Eternal was ever the One God, the True God; and Moses his interpreter. Moral and social disorder had invaded the Hebrew Confederation; the Divine Law and Tradition were incessantly violated, still not ignored: they ever continued the Divine Law and Tradition, the objects of the faith and veneration of Israel.

When the evil of anarchy had brought with it great national reverses,—when the Philistines on the south, the Ammonites on the east, and the Mesopotamians on the north, had placed in jeopardy the Hebrew settlement in Canaan,—a general cry arose; on all sides, the tribes demanded a strong government, a single chief, one capable of maintaining order within, and supporting abroad the position and the honour of Israel. A great and faithful servant of Jehovah, the last of the judges, and the greatest of the prophets since Moses,—Samuel,—had recently governed Israel, and strenuously struggled to arrest the progress of popular vice and misfortune; but he had become old, and his sons whom he had made "judges over Israel ... walked not in his ways, but turned aside after lucre, and took bribes, and perverted judgment. Then all the elders of Israel gathered themselves together, and came to Samuel unto Ramah, and said unto him, Behold, thou art old, and thy sons walk not in thy ways: now make us a king to judge us like all the nations." [Footnote 61]

[Footnote 61: 1 Samuel viii. 1-5.]

The demand had in it nothing singular; even at the epoch when God, by his servant Moses, was personally governing Israel, the chance of the establishment of a human kingdom had been foreseen and provided for beforehand by the Divine Law: "When thou art come unto the land which the Lord thy God giveth thee, and shalt possess it, and shalt dwell therein, and shalt say, I will set a king over me, like as all the nations that are about me; thou shalt in any wise set him king over thee, whom the Lord thy God shall choose: one from among thy brethren shalt thou set king over thee: thou mayest not set a stranger over thee, which is not thy brother." [Footnote 62]

[Footnote 62: Deuteronomy xvii. 14, 15.]

Although thus provided for by the Divine Law, the demand of a king was extremely displeasing to Samuel; "for the kingly rule was odious to him," says the historian Josephus; "he had an innate love of justice, and was ardently attached to the aristocratical form of government, as to the form of polity which rendered men happy and worthy of God." [Footnote 63]

[Footnote 63: Josephus, Ant. Jud. vol. vi. ch. iii. 3.]

But the Eternal "said unto Samuel, Hearken unto the voice of the people in all that they say unto thee: for they have not rejected thee, but they have rejected me, that I should not reign over them ... Now therefore hearken unto their voice; howbeit yet protest solemnly unto them, and shew them the manner of the king that shall reign over them." [Footnote 64]

[Footnote 64: 1 Samuel viii. 7-9.]

Samuel predicted to the Hebrews how much the kingly form of government would cost them, all that they would have to suffer in their families, their property, and their liberties: "Nevertheless the people refused to obey the voice of Samuel; and they said, Nay; but we will have a king over us; that we also may be like all the nations; and that our king may judge us, and go out before us, and fight our battles. And Samuel heard all the words of the people, and he rehearsed them in the ears of the Lord. And the Lord said to Samuel, Hearken unto their voice, and make them a king." [Footnote 65]

[Footnote 65: 1 Samuel viii. 19-22.]

The world's history offers no example where the merits and defects of absolute monarchy were so rapidly developed, where they were displayed so strikingly, as in this little Hebrew monarchy, instituted with the view of escaping from anarchy by the express desire of the people itself. Three kings succeed to the throne, in origin, character, conduct, and reign absolutely dissimilar. Saul is a warrior, chosen by Samuel for his strength, bodily beauty, and courage; ever ready for the combat, but without foresight, without perseverance in his military operations; easily intoxicated with good fortune; hurried away by brutal, capricious, or jealous passions; now engaged in furious struggles, now appearing in a dependent position, with his patron Samuel, his son Jonathan, his son-in-law David; a genuine barbarian king, arrogant, changeable of humour, impatient of control, prone to superstition, a moment serving Israel against her enemies, but incapable of governing Israel in the name of its God.

David, on the contrary, is the faithful and consistent representative of religious faith and religious life in Israel; the fervent and submissive adorer of the Eternal; he is so at all the epochs and in the most varying aspects of his career, whether of humility or of grandeur; at once warrior, king, prophet, poet; as ardent to celebrate his God in his character of poet, as to serve Him in the capacity of warrior, or to obey Him in that of king; equally sublime in his thanksgiving to the Eternal for his triumphs as in his invocation to Him in his distresses; accessible to the most culpable human weaknesses, but prompt to repent the offence once committed; and giving always to impulses of joy or pious sadness the first place in his soul; very king of the nation that adores the very God. David accomplishes the work of his time: he obtains the object for which the monarchy had been demanded and instituted: he leaves behind him the tribes of Israel reunited at home, and reassured against foreign enemies, proceeding too in the path of good order and confidence. Heir to his father's work, his father's success, Solomon comes next, and reigns forty years—years of almost as much repose as splendour: "God gave Solomon wisdom and understanding exceeding much, and largeness of heart, even as the sand that is on the sea shore." [Footnote 66] "And he had peace on all sides round about him. And Judah and Israel dwelt safely, every man under his vine and under his fig tree, from Dan even to Beersheba, all the days of Solomon." [Footnote 67]

[Footnote 66: 1 Kings iv. 29.]

[USCCB: Footnote 66 should be: 1 Kings iv. 9.]

[Footnote 67: Ibid. 24, 25.]

[USCCB: Footnote 67 should be: 1 Kings iv. 4, 5.]

The kingdom and the kingly authority rose under the government of Solomon, and throughout all Western Asia, to a degree of power and splendour before unknown to the Hebrews. A prosperity out of all proportion with the position of a new king and a small state, and which reminds us of the rapid histories and the political comets of the East. Solomon at this point lost sight of both wisdom and virtue: the first hereditary prince of the Hebrew monarchy terminated his life like a voluptuous sovereign of Ecbatana or of Nineveh; the son of the pious King David became a sceptical moralist; although a profound observer of the nature and destiny of man, such observation had led but to feelings of disgust. Nor did the monarchy survive the monarch: the nation became effeminate and corrupt, in the effeminacy and corruption of its sovereign. Scarcely was Solomon dead, when his monarchy was divided into two kingdoms, which, at first rivals, became soon openly hostile to each other; sometimes a prey to tyranny, sometimes to anarchy, and almost always to war. It was not, as formerly, merely a bad phase of transition in the history of the Hebrew nation; it was the commencement of national decline—decline irremediable, hopeless.

But what, in this decline, will become of the law revealed on Sinai to Moses? Is it destined to fall with the monarchy of Solomon, or to languish and die out in the midst of the struggles and disasters of Judah and of Israel? Quite the contrary: the religious faith and law of the Hebrews will not only perpetuate themselves, but will again shine forth at this epoch of political ruin.

Above the fortune of states are the designs of God, to which instruments are never wanting; the kings continue to perpetrate acts of violence, and the people to show marks of weakness; but amidst all, the prophets of Israel will maintain the ancient Covenant, and prepare the coming of that new Covenant which is to make of the God of Israel the God of mankind.

IV. God And The Prophets.

A celebrated political writer—a freethinker belonging to the Radical school, somewhat also to the school of Positivism—Mr. John Stuart Mill, has recently said, in his work on Government, "The Egyptian hierarchy, the paternal despotism of China, were very fit instruments for carrying those nations up to the point of civilisation which they attained. But, having reached that point, they were brought to a permanent halt, for want of mental liberty and individuality; requisites of improvement which the institutions that had carried them thus far, entirely incapacitated them from acquiring; and, as the institutions did not break down and give place to others, further improvement stopped. In contrast with these nations, let us consider the example of an opposite character afforded by another and a comparatively insignificant Oriental people—the Jews. They, too, had an absolute monarchy and a hierarchy, and their organised institutions were as obviously of sacerdotal origin as those of the Hindoos. These did for them what was done for other Oriental races by their institutions—subdued them to industry and order, and gave them a national life. But neither their kings nor their priests ever obtained, as in those other countries, the exclusive moulding of their character. Their religion, which enabled persons of genius and a high religious tone to be regarded and to regard themselves as inspired from Heaven, gave existence to an inestimably precious unorganized institution—the Order (if it may be so termed) of Prophets. Generally under the protection—it was not always effectual—of their sacred character, the prophets were a power in the nation, often more than a match for kings and priests, and kept up in that little corner of the earth the antagonism of influence, which is the only real security for continued progress. Religion consequently was not there—what it has been in so many other places—a consecration of all that was once established, and a barrier against further improvement. The remark of a distinguished Hebrew, M. Salvador, that the prophets were, in Church and State, the equivalent to the modern liberty of the press, gives a just but not an adequate conception of the part fulfilled in national and universal histories by this great element of Jewish life; by means of which, the canon of inspiration never being complete, the persons most eminent in genius and moral feeling could not only denounce and reprobate, with the direct authority of the Almighty, whatever appeared to them deserving of such treatment, but could give forth better and higher interpretations of the national religion. Conditions more favourable to progress could not easily exist; accordingly the Jews, instead of being stationary like other Asiatics, were, next to the Greeks, the most progressive people of antiquity, and, jointly with them, have been the starting-point and main propelling agency of modern cultivation." [Footnote 68]

> [Footnote 68: Considerations on Representative Government. By John Stuart Mill, pp. 41-43. London.]

Mr. Mill is right, only he does not go far enough. Modern civilization is in effect derived from the Jews and from the Greeks. To the latter it is indebted for its human and intellectual, to the former for its Divine and moral, element. Of these two sources, we owe to the Jews, if not the more brilliant, at all events the more sublime and dearly acquired one. After the development of power and grandeur which took place amongst the Jews in the reigns of David and Solomon, their history is but a long series of misfortunes and reverses,—an eventful, painful decline. The Hebrew state is divided into two kingdoms, almost constantly at war with each other. And whilst the kingdom of Israel is a prey to continual usurpations and revolutions, making it the scene of all the violence and all the vicissitudes of a tyranny, the kingdom of Judah has a line of princes, in turn good or bad, who keep it unceasingly in a state of trouble and of jeopardy. Religion falls beneath the yoke of secular government; idolatry appears in the kingdom of Israel, and braves audaciously the ancient national faith. The kingdom of Judah, however, remains more faithful to Jehovah and his law, to the traditions of Moses, and to the race of David; but its languishing faith is no longer strong enough to arrest its march in the path of decline. In the two kingdoms, internal disorders are aggravated by reverses abroad; in the meantime, around them mighty empires spring up and succeed to each other. First Israel and then Judah are invaded by strangers; they are subjugated in turn by the Assyrians, the Egyptians, the Syrians, the Babylonians. The Hebrews are not only vanquished and reduced to subjection, but exiled, transported, led captive far from their country. A new conqueror, Cyrus, permits them to return to Jerusalem; but not to resume their independence; at first subjects of the Persian kings, they soon pass from their empire to that of the Greek generals, who have divided amongst one another the conquests of Alexander; then to the rule of the Greeks succeeds that of the Romans. During this succession of servitudes, scarcely are they allowed any moments of existence as a free nation, and even this freedom is more apparent than real. Judea, like Greece, is subjugated, but under circumstances of greater humiliation and distress.

And shall, then, the Hebrews oppose no efficacious resistance to these reverses? What is to become, in this absolute ruin of the nationality of the Jews, of their God, and their faith? Shall the miracles of Sinai have no more virtue than the mysteries of Eleusis, and Jehovah languish away and vanish in the routine of sacerdotal ceremonies, or in philosophical scepticism?

By no means: in the midst of his people's decay, the God of Israel maintains interpreters who struggle with indomitable fidelity against public calamities and popular errors. The first of the prophets, Moses, had spoken in the name and according to the commandment of Jehovah. After him there never were wanting to Israel men who inherited or pretended to the heritage of the same Divine mission. "I will raise them up a Prophet from among their brethren, like unto thee," said the Eternal unto Moses, "and will put my words in his mouth; and he shall speak unto them all that I shall command him. ... But the prophet, which shall presume to speak a word in my name, which I have not commanded him to speak, or that shall speak in the name of other gods, even that prophet shall die." [Footnote 69]

[Footnote 69: Deuteronomy xviii. 18, 20.]

From Moses to Samuel, the series of the prophets is continued; some of them are of renown, like Nathan in the reigns of David and Solomon; but the greater number, without name in history, and appearing scattered over a long course of years. They are called the ***Seers***, [Footnote 70] or the Inspired. [Footnote 71]

[Footnote 70: Roêh or Chozeh, in Hebrew.]

[Footnote 71: Nabi.]

Their speech gushes forth like a well under the breath of God. When the government of the Judges gives place to that of the Kings, the great actor in this drama of transition, Samuel, opens for the prophets a new era; dedicated from his infancy to God's service, he feels beforehand and abides the divine inspiration: "Speak, Lord; for thy servant heareth." [Footnote 72]

[Footnote 72: 1 Samuel iii. 9, 10.]

Not long after, his renown spreads amongst the people; he is not pontiff, he is not even priest. [Footnote 73]

[Footnote 73: Samuel propheta fuit, judex fuit, levita fuit, non pontifex, ne saoerdos quidem.—St. Jerom adv. Jovinianum.]

But he is pre-eminently the seer: "Is not the seer here?" Such is the question addressed to some young maidens by the men who are in search of Samuel. Saul meets him without knowing him, and says to him, "I pray thee tell me where the house of the seer is." "I am the seer," replied Samuel; and soon after, it is Samuel himself, who, in compliance with the popular vote, approved by God, proclaims Saul king. But at the moment when he thus changes the theocracy in Israel into a monarchy, he foresees the vices and perils attendant upon the new government, and opposes to them the element of resistance drawn from their national beliefs and traditions; he transforms the order of prophets into a permanent institution; he founds schools of prophets, independent servants of Jehovah, consecrated to the defence of his law and the enunciation of his will; constituting a sort of congregation independent of both Church and State; leading, in fixed and appointed places,—at Rama, Bethel, Jericho, Jerusalem,—a life in common, but with out exclusive privileges; the sons of the prophets are brought up near their fathers; but still the mission of prophecy is accessible to all who have the call from God: "Go, thou seer," said the priest Amaziah, in his anger, to the prophet Amos, "flee thee away into the land of Judah, and there eat bread, and prophesy there: but prophesy not again any more at Bethel: for it is the king's chapel, and it is the king's court. Then answered Amos, and said to Amaziah, I was no prophet, neither was I a prophet's son: but I was a herdman, and a gatherer of sycomore fruit: and the Eternal took me as I followed the flock, and the Lord said unto me, Go, prophesy unto my people Israel." [Footnote 74]

[Footnote 74: Amos vii. 12-15.]

The prophets are neither priests nor monks: sprung from all the classes of the Jewish nation, their vocation is essentially independent. They belong to God alone, and await divine inspiration to oppose, as it may happen, at one time the tyranny of the kings, at another the passions of the populace, at another the corruption of the priesthood: their only arms, the commands of God and the gift of prophecy. The functions assigned to them are as different as the places and circumstances of their life; but they are ready to take any part and to encounter any peril: some of them, like Elijah and Elisha, are men of action and of combat; the others, like Isaiah, Jeremiah, Ezekiel, Amos, are narrators, moralists, prophets; some devote themselves to attacks upon the acts of violence and impiety committed by the kings, the others to the vices and corruption of the people; the same spirit, however, animates them all; they are all interpreters and labourers of Jehovah; they defend, all of them, the faith of God against idolatry, justice and right against tyranny, the national independence against foreign dominion. In the name of the God of Abraham and of Jacob, they labour and succeed in maintaining or in reanimating religious and moral life amidst the decay and servitude of Israel. "All the time," says St. Augustine, "from the epoch when the holy Samuel began to prophesy, to the day when the people of Israel was led captive into Babylonia, is the period of the prophets." [Footnote 75]

[Footnote 75: De Civitate Dei, l. xvii. ch. 1.]

To accomplish their mission, to ensure their hard-earned successes, they had other arms than lamentations and exhortations, arising out of what was past and inevitable; other expedients than pious reproaches and expressions of regret. These defenders of the ancient faith of Moses do not shut themselves up within the external forms and rites of their religion; they pursue the moral object that it proposes; they insist upon the spirit that vivifies it. "Your new moons and your appointed feasts my soul hateth" (said the Lord, according to Isaiah): "they are a trouble unto me; I am weary to bear them. And when ye spread forth your hands, I will hide mine eyes from you: yea, when ye make many prayers, I will not hear: your hands are full of blood. Wash you, make you clean; put away the evil of your doings from before mine eyes; cease to do evil; learn to do well; seek judgment, relieve the oppressed, judge the fatherless, plead for the widow." [Footnote 76]

[Footnote 76: Isaiah i. 14-17.]

"Wherewith shall I come before the Lord" (said the prophet Micah), "and bow myself before the high God? shall I come before him with burnt offerings, with calves of a year old? Will the Lord be pleased with thousands of rams, or with ten thousands of rivers of oil? shall I give my firstborn for my transgression, the fruit of my body for the sin of my soul? He hath shewed thee, O man, what is good; and what doth the Lord require of thee, but to do justly, and to love mercy, and to walk humbly with thy God?" [Footnote 77]

[Footnote 77: Micah vi. 6-8.]

Even whilst calling the people of Israel back to the faith of their fathers, the prophets open to them new perspectives: whilst reproaching them with the errors that have led to their decay and servitude, they permit them yet to see the future delivery and regeneration. It is their divine character to live at once in the past and in the future; to confide alike to the ordinances of the Eternal and to his promises: they move forward, but they change not; they believe, they hope; they are faithful to Moses whilst they announce the Messiah.

V. Expectation Of The Messiah.

Controversy has the mischievous power of the Homeric Jupiter: it collects clouds amidst which the light that we seek for disappears.

The Old and the New Testament, the history of the Jews and the history of Jesus Christ, lie before us. Do these two monuments form but one single edifice? That second history, is it comprised and written beforehand in the first? Such is the question which has for the last eighteen centuries occupied and divided the learned. Some affirm that Jesus Christ was foreseen and predicted among the Jews, and that the series of prophecies continued from the very time of Moses until the advent of Christ. Others lay stress upon the hiatus—the want of connection and cohesion—the contradictions to be detected here between the Old and New Testament; and thence they conclude that the text of the Old Testament by no means contains the facts that appear in the New Testament, and that the miraculous history of Jesus Christ was, in the bosom of Israel, neither miraculously foreseen nor predicted.

Why was it, and how was it possible, that two assertions so contradictory came to be both adopted and maintained by men most of them as sincere as learned?

They have all committed the fault of plunging into the petty details of facts and texts, searching in all places, without exception, for the complete demonstration of their particular theses, and losing sight of the great fact, the general and dominant fact to which we should refer as alone capable of solving the question. They descend into the mazy paths which perplex the plain below, instead of grasping from the summit of the mountains, the whole comprehensive view, and the grand road leading to the goal itself. Believers have insisted upon discovering, fact by fact, in the biblical prophecies the whole mission and all the life of Jesus. The incredulous, on the other hand, have minutely adverted to all the discrepancies, all the difficulties, suggested by a comparison of the texts of the Old Testament and of the Gospel narrative; they have contrasted the glories of the Messiah, the powerful King of Israel, so often announced by the prophets, with the humble life, the cruel death of Jesus, and with the ruin of Jerusalem. In my opinion, they have on both sides lost sight of the inward and essential characteristic of this sublime history; the special action of God is revealed therein, but without suppressing the action of men; miracles take their place in the midst of the natural course of events; the ambitious aspirations of the Jews connect themselves with the religious perspective opened to them by the prophets; the divine and the human, the inspiration from on high and the impulse of the national imagination, appear together. These two elements should be disentangled: the mind should be raised above the perplexing influences which they exercise, and the attention directed to that heavenly beam which pierces the vapours of this earthly atmosphere. Thus, all the embarrassment that controversy occasioned vanishing, the history yields to us its profound meanings, and, in spite of complications having their origin in the wordy explanations of man, the design of God makes itself manifest in all its majestic simplicity.

Discarding all discussion and commentary, let us merely collect, from epoch to epoch, the principal texts which speak of the advent of the future Messiah. I might here multiply citations, but I limit myself to those where the allusion is evident. It is the Bible, and the Bible alone, that is speaking.

The first act of disobedience to God, the act of original sin, has just been committed. The Eternal God says to the serpent that has seduced Eve: "Because thou hast done this, thou art cursed above all cattle, and above every beast of the field. ... And I will put enmity between thee and the woman, and between thy seed and her seed; it shall bruise thy head, and thou shalt bruise his heel." [Footnote 78]

[Footnote 78: Genesis iii. 14, 15.]

He that shall bruise the head of the serpent shall belong, says the Book of Genesis, to the race of Shem, to the posterity of Abraham and Jacob, to the kingdom of Judah. "But thou, Beth-lehem Ephratah, though thou be little among the thousands of Judah, yet out of thee shall he come forth unto me that is to be Ruler in Israel." [Footnote 79]

[Footnote 79: Genesis ix. 26; xii. 3; xlix. 10; Micah v. 2.]

Israel is at its apogee of splendour: David prophesies alike the sufferings and the glory of that Saviour of the world who is to be not merely the King of Zion, but "the Son and the Anointed of the Eternal:" "My God, my God, why hast thou forsaken me?" is the expression attributed to him by the prophet king. ... "All they that see me laugh me to scorn: they shoot out the lip, they shake the head. ... They gave me also gall for my meat, and in my thirst they gave me vinegar to drink. ... They part my garments among them, and cast lots upon my vesture. ... He trusted on the Lord that he would deliver him; let him deliver him, seeing he delighted in him. ... Ye that fear the Lord, praise him; all ye the seed of Jacob, glorify him; and fear him, all ye the seed of Israel. ... All the ends of the earth shall remember and turn unto the Lord: and all the kindreds of the nations shall worship before thee." [Footnote 80]

> [Footnote 80: Psalms ii. 2, 6, 7; xxii. 1, 7; lxix. 21; xxii. 18, 8, 23, 27.]

The kingdom of David and of Solomon has begun to decay; Judah and Israel are separating; both kingdoms have their prophets, who at one time struggle against the crimes and evils of their respective ages, and, at another, occupy themselves in disclosing prospects of the future.

> "Hear ye now, O house of David. ...
>
> "Therefore the Lord himself shall give you a sign; Behold, a virgin shall conceive, and bear a son, and shall call his name Immanuel. ...
>
> "The people that walked in darkness have seen a great light: they that dwell in the land of the shadow of death, upon them hath the light shined. ...
>
> "For unto us a child is born, unto us a son is given: and the government shall be upon his shoulder: and his name shall be called Wonderful, Counsellor, The mighty God, The everlasting Father, The Prince of Peace. ...
> "And there shall come forth a rod out of the stem of Jesse, and a Branch shall grow out of his roots:
>
> "And the spirit of the Lord shall rest upon him, the spirit of wisdom and understanding, the spirit of counsel and might, the spirit of knowledge and of the fear of the Lord;
>
> "... and he shall not judge after the sight of his eyes, neither reprove

after the hearing of his ears:

"But with righteousness shall he judge the poor, and reprove with equity, for the meek of the earth. …

"Listen, O isles, unto me; and hearken, ye people, from far; The Lord hath called me from the womb; from the bowels of my mother hath he made mention of my name. …

"And said unto me, Thou art my servant, O Israel, in whom I will be glorified.

"Then I said, I have laboured in vain, I have spent my strength for nought, and in vain: yet surely my judgment is with the Lord, and my work with my God.

"And now, saith the Lord that formed me from the womb to be his servant, to bring Jacob again to him, Though Israel be not gathered, yet shall I be glorious in the eyes of the Lord, and my God shall be my strength.

"And he said, It is a light thing that thou shouldest be my servant to raise up the tribes of Jacob, and to restore the preserved of Israel: I will also give thee for a light to the Gentiles, that thou mayest be my salvation unto the end of the earth. …

"Rejoice greatly, O daughter of Zion; shout, O daughter of Jerusalem: behold, thy King cometh unto thee: he is just, and having salvation; lowly, and riding upon an ass, and upon a colt the foal of an ass.

"… For he shall grow up before him as a tender plant, and as a root out of a dry ground: he hath no form nor comeliness; and when we shall see him, there is no beauty that we should desire him.

"He is despised and rejected of men; a man of sorrows, and acquainted with grief: and we hid as it were our faces from him; he was despised, and we esteemed him not.

"Surely he hath borne our griefs, and carried our sorrows: yet we did esteem him stricken, smitten of God, and afflicted.

"But he was wounded for our trangressions, he was bruised for our iniquities: the chastisement of our peace was upon him; and with his stripes we are healed.

"All we like sheep have gone astray; we have turned every one to his own way; and the Lord hath laid on him the iniquity of us all.

"He was oppressed, and he was afflicted, yet he opened not his mouth: he is brought as a lamb to the slaughter, and as a sheep before her shearers is dumb, so he openeth not his mouth.

"He was taken from prison and from judgment: and who shall declare his generation? for he was cut off out of the land of the living: for the transgression of my people was he stricken. ...

"Yet it pleased the Lord to bruise him; he hath put him to grief: when thou shalt make his soul an offering for sin, he shall see his seed, he shall prolong his days, and the pleasure of the Lord shall prosper in his hand.

"He shall see of the travail of his soul, and shall be satisfied: by his knowledge shall my righteous servant justify many; for he shall bear their iniquities.

"Therefore will I divide him a portion with the great, and he shall divide the spoil with the strong; because he hath poured out his soul unto death: and he was numbered with the transgressors; and he bare the sin of many, and made intercession for the transgressors." [Footnote 81]

[Footnote 81: Isaiah vii. 13-14; ix. 26; xi. 14; xlix. 1-6; Zechariah ix. 9; Isaiah liii.]

Whatever controversies may arise out of these texts, and many others which I might cite, one fact subsists and rises above all question and all controversy. Seventeen centuries passed in the interval between the Decalogue being received by Moses upon Mount Sinai, and the actual approach of the Messiah announced by the prophets; and at the end of these seventeen centuries, the God, from whom Moses received the Decalogue, He who defined himself to be "I am that I am." Jehovah, still is, has never ceased to be the God, the sole God of Israel. Israel has passed through all governments, undergone all vicissitudes, fallen into all the errors to which it is possible for a nation to succumb: the Jews have had a hierarchy, and judges, and kings; they have been alternately conquerors and conquered, masters and slaves; they have had their days of power and their days of humiliation, their temptation to idolatry and paroxysms of impiety; still they have ever returned to the One God: to the true God; their faith has survived all their faults and all their misfortunes; and after those seventeen centuries, Israel is waiting at the hand of Jehovah a Messiah, to be, according to the affirmation of its greatest prophets, the Liberator and the Saviour, not of Israel alone, but of all nations. Fact without parallel in history! In vain shall men exhaust against it all their science, and all their scepticism: there is here more than the work of man; the fact itself is not human. But what more shall that fact become, and what shall be our belief, when all shall have received its consummation,—the prophecies their accomplishment,—when Jehovah shall have given to the world Jesus Christ?

Eighth Meditation.
Jesus Christ According To The Gospel.

Need I say that by the words, "the Gospel," here used, I understand the four Gospels, the Acts of the Apostles, the Epistles, all the books, in fact, which compose the Canon of the New Testament as it is received by all Christians?

These books have been variously studied: now with the design of disproving, now of explaining the life of Jesus Christ; now with the object of a Controversialist, now with that of a Commentator. I approach the subject in neither character. I would wish to study Jesus Christ in the New Testament solely to know Him well, and to make Him well known; to place Him before the reader, and to depict Him faithfully according to the evidence of his history. I propose hereafter, in a second series of these ***Meditations***, to examine its authenticity, and the degree of credit to which it is entitled. For the moment I assume the testimony as good and valid. Beyond all doubt, at the outset, it is at least entitled to this respect. The powerful influence of these books, and of the accounts which they contain, such as they remain to us, has been put to the test and proved. They have overcome Paganism. They have conquered Greece, Rome, and barbarous Europe. They are actually overcoming the world. And the sincerity of the authors is no less certain than the virtue of the books: however possible it may be to contest the enlightenment, the critical sagacity of the original historians of Jesus Christ, their good faith is beyond all question: it appears in their language; they believed what they said; they sealed their assertions with their blood: "I believe," said Pascal, "only those histories, the witnesses to which confirm their attestation by submitting to death." Although not always a sufficient reason to believe an account, it constitutes a decisive motive to believe in the sincerity of the witness.

I have before cited from the Old Testament some of the texts which contain the promises made to Israel of the Messiah. These promises had evidently excited lively attention amongst the Jews; the satisfaction felt at their accomplishment expressed itself loudly at the birth of Jesus Christ: "And behold, there was a man in Jerusalem, whose name was Simeon ... waiting for the consolation of Israel: and the Holy Ghost was upon him. ... Lord, now lettest thou thy servant depart in peace, according to thy word: For mine eyes have seen thy salvation, which thou hast prepared before the face of all people; a light to lighten the Gentiles, and the glory of thy people Israel." [Footnote 82]

[Footnote 82: Luke ii. 25-32.]

Besides Simeon, a pious woman, Anna, "of about fourscore and four years, which departed not from the temple, but served God with fastings and prayers night and day. And she coming in that instant gave thanks unto the Lord, and spake of him to all them that looked for redemption in Jerusalem." [Footnote 83]

[Footnote 83: Luke ii. 37, 38.]

But there was far more than merely the demonstrations of Simeon and Anna,—than these impulses of joy on the part of the faithful followers of Jehovah: "In those days came John the Baptist, preaching in the wilderness of Judæa. ... And the same John had his raiment of camel's hair, and a leathern girdle about his loins; and his meat was locusts and wild honey. ... And saying, Repent ye, for the kingdom of heaven is at hand. For this is he that was spoken of by the prophet Esaias, saying, The voice of one crying in the wilderness, Prepare ye the way of the Lord, make his paths straight. ... I indeed baptize you with water unto repentance. ... But there standeth one among you, whom ye know not. He it is who, coming after me, is preferred before me, whose shoe's latchet I am not worthy to unloose. ... And I knew him not: but that he should be made manifest to Israel, therefore am I come baptizing with water. ... And I saw, and bare record that this is the Son of God." [Footnote 84]

[Footnote 84: Matthew iii. 1-5; Mark i. 2-11; Luke iii. 1-18; John i. 26-34.]

Attempts have sometimes been made, although with no very great confidence on the part of the propounders of the theory, to represent Jesus as the most eminent among several reformers, who, about the same epoch, aspired to the title and character of the Messiah predicted by the prophets and expected by Israel. Reference has been particularly made to one of His predecessors, Judas the Gaulonite, who, a few years after the birth of Jesus, on the occasion of a census ordered by the Imperial Legate Quirinius, undertook to raise Judæa in insurrection against this measure—against the tribute that it imposed, and against the Emperor himself—proclaiming that to God alone belonged the appellation ***Master***, and that liberty was worth more than life. [Footnote 85]

[Footnote 85: Joseph. Antiq. Jud. 1. xvii. ch. 6; 1. xviii. ch. 1. Acts of the Apostles, ch. v. 34-39.]

These comparisons—I forbear to use the word assimilations—are entirely without foundation. These men, who, as it is pretended, anticipated the career of Jesus, were simply men who opposed the Roman dominion, and who stood up, like the Maccabees before them, in the name of national independence, and in a spirit of reaction in favor of the Mosaic government. Jesus was not so anticipated: His mission had no relation with any previous essay; and his sole forerunner was John the Baptist, as strange as himself to any political view or conspiracy, and as humble before Him—before the true, the sole Messiah—as Judas the Gaulonite and his adherents were bold and daring towards the Emperor.

There is an interval of thirty years between the birth of Jesus and the day when He enters actively on the performance of his divine mission. [Footnote 86]

> [Footnote 86: The question as to the precise epoch of the birth of Jesus Christ, as well as of the commencement and the duration of His public career, has been well and concisely considered in the Synopsis Evangelica of M. Constantin Tischendorf (p. 16-19. Leipzig, 1864). The preferable conclusion from these researches is, that Jesus Christ was born in the year of Roma 750, that he commenced his divine mission towards the end of the year of Rome 780, and that his death took place in the fourth month of the year of Rome 783.]

These thirty years, however, were not idly passed, nor were they without their peculiar testimony to Christ and the future in store for Him:—

> "And Joseph and his mother marvelled at those things which were spoken of him. …
>
> "And the child grew, and waxed strong in spirit, filled with wisdom: and the grace of God was upon him.
>
> "Now his parents went to Jerusalem every year at the feast of the Passover.
>
> "And when he was twelve years old, they went up to Jerusalem after the custom of the feast.
>
> "And when they had fulfilled the days, as they returned, the child Jesus tarried behind in Jerusalem; and Joseph and his mother knew

not of it.

"But they, supposing him to have been in the company, went a day's journey; and they sought him among their kinsfolk and acquaintance.

"And when they found him not, they turned back again to Jerusalem, seeking him.

"And it came to pass, that after three days they found him in the temple, sitting in the midst of the doctors, both hearing them, and asking them questions.

"And all that heard him were astonished at his understanding and answers.

"And when they saw him, they were amazed: and his mother said unto him, Son, why hast thou thus dealt with us? Behold, thy father and I have sought thee sorrowing.

"And he said unto them, How is it that ye sought me? wist ye not that I must be about my Father's business?

"And they understood not the saying which he spake unto them.

"And he went down with them, and came to Nazareth, and was subject unto them: but his mother kept all these sayings in her heart.

"And Jesus increased in wisdom and stature, and in favour with God and man." [Footnote 87]

[Footnote 87: Luke ii. 33, 40-52.]

Thus begins that manifestation in the person of the child Jesus Christ, that mixture of humanity and divinity, of natural life and miraculous life, which is his peculiar and sublime characteristic. In the opinion of the men who, in principle, reject the supernatural, this mixed divine-human nature, and consequently Jesus Christ himself, is at once incomprehensible and inadmissible. What wonder if Christ has in these days to encounter such adversaries? Had He not to do so when invested with the attributes of humanity, among contemporaries, and even in his own family? In his first days of human existence, his mother, Mary, saw Him and understood Him not. And nevertheless "Mary kept all these sayings in her heart." Expression, at once profound and touching; revealing the mysterious complication of the nature of man! Man is not content to resign himself to the limits imposed by the actual laws of the finite world; his aspirations tend elsewhere. And still, when called upon to rise above the present order of nature—that order which he is able to appreciate—he experiences a certain astonishment, a certain hesitation; he does not know if he ought to believe in that supernatural that he was recently invoking, and that he never ceases to invoke; for, like Mary, he preserves the instinct in his heart! It is just at the present day as it was nineteen centuries ago. Jesus has ever to encounter such contradictory moods of human nature: He is confronted at once by the hope of, the thirsting after, the supernatural inherent in the human soul, and by all the objections, all the doubts that the supernatural itself suggests to the human mind. He has to satisfy that hope, to surmount those doubts. The Gospel opens the history of this solemn struggle, that gave rise to Christianity, and is the source of all those agitations which afflict Christians at the present day.

I. Jesus Christ And His Apostles.

On entering upon the active purposes of his mission, it is the will of Jesus to have, and He has Disciples—Apostles. He knows the power of an association founded upon faith and love. He knows also that faith and love are virtues as rare as they are efficacious. It is not numbers that He seeks. He surrounds himself with a select band of believers, and lives with them in a complete and enduring intimacy.

In the midst of these intimate relations, Jesus declares his authority primitive and supreme:—"Ye have not chosen me, but I have chosen you, and ordained you, that ye should go and bring forth fruit." [Footnote 88]

[Footnote 88: John xv. 16.]

But the authority of the Master does not prevent Him from evincing a tenderness full of trust, and from respecting himself the dignity of his disciples:—"Henceforth I call you not servants; for the servant knoweth not what his lord doeth: but I have called you friends; for all things that I have heard of my Father I have made known unto you." [Footnote 89]

[Footnote 89: John xv. 15.]

He evinces on all occasions towards his apostles the trust that He feels in them, and shows his sense of the superiority of the position to which He has elevated them. His language sometimes fills them with astonishment, and they are more peculiarly struck by the numerous parables in which, whilst addressing the assembled multitude, He clothes his precepts:—"And the disciples came, and said unto him, Why speakest thou unto them in parables? He answered and said unto them, Because it is given unto you to know the mysteries of the kingdom of heaven, but to them it is not given. … But unto those that are without, all these things are done in parables." [Footnote 90]

[Footnote 90: Matthew xiii. 10, 11; Mark iv. 10, 11.]

The confidingness of Jesus, however, never descends to weak compliance; when, in an impulse of vanity and ambition, one of his apostles asks for a particular favour, Jesus rebukes him with severity:—"James and John, the sons of Zebedee, come unto him, saying, Master, we would that thou shouldest do for us whatsoever we shall desire. And he said unto them, What would ye that I should do for you? They said unto him, Grant unto us that we may sit, one on thy right hand, and the other on thy left hand, in thy glory. But Jesus said unto them, Ye know not what ye ask: can ye drink of the cup that I drink of? and be baptized with the baptism that I am baptized with? And they said unto him, We can. And Jesus said unto them, Ye shall indeed drink of the cup that I drink of; and with the baptism that I am baptized withal shall ye be baptized: But to sit on my right hand and on my left hand is not mine to give; but it shall be given to them for whom it is prepared. … Ye know that they which are accounted to rule over the Gentiles exercise lordship over them; and their great ones exercise authority upon them. But so shall it not be among you: but whosoever will be great among you, shall be your minister." [Footnote 91]

[Footnote 91: Mark x. 35-43; Matthew xx. 20-26.]

Jesus having thus selected and intimately attached to Him his apostles, commissions them to carry forth his law:—"Go not into the way of the Gentiles, and into any city of the Samaritans enter ye not: But go rather to the lost sheep of the house of Israel. And as ye go, preach, saying, The kingdom of heaven is at hand. Heal the sick, cleanse the lepers, raise the dead, cast out devils: freely ye have received, freely give. Provide neither gold, nor silver, nor brass in your purses, nor scrips for your journey, neither two coats, neither shoes, nor yet staves: for the workman is worthy of his meat. … Behold, I send ye forth as sheep in the midst of wolves: be ye therefore wise as serpents and harmless as doves." [Footnote 92]

[Footnote 92: Matthew x. 5-10, 16; Luke x. 1-12.]

It is, in effect, prudence side by side with absolute self-denegation that Jesus, in his first instructions, enjoins upon his disciples; at the very commencement of their mission He limits its object; He recommends to them particularly "the lost sheep of the house of Israel;" He declares his will to be that, instead of a pertinacity with out bounds, "they should depart, shaking off the dust from their feet, out of the city that should not receive them nor hear their words." But He adds immediately, as if to give to their mission all its grandeur:—"What I tell you in darkness, that speak ye in light: and what ye hear in the ear, that preach ye upon the house-tops. And fear not them which kill the body, but are not able to kill the soul: but rather fear him which is able to destroy both soul and body in hell." [Footnote 93]

[Footnote 93: Matthew x. 27, 28.]

Jesus knows that his disciples will need the firmest courage, and, far from promising them any of the goods of this world, any temporal successes, He discloses to them unceasingly all the perils they will incur, all the invectives they will have to endure. "But beware of men: for they will deliver you up to the councils, and they will scourge you in their synagogues; and ye shall be brought before governors and kings for my sake, for a testimony against them and the Gentiles ... And ye shall be betrayed both by parents, and brethren, and kinsfolks and friends; and some of you shall they cause to be put to death. And ye shall be hated of all men for my name's sake." [Footnote 94]

[Footnote 94: Matthew x. 17-22. Luke xxi. 12-17.]

What Reformer, other than Jesus Christ, ever held to his followers such language? Who else than God could have imparted to their language such virtue that they would in obedience to it sacrifice with joy not merely all the good things of this life, but life itself? Nevertheless, one of those apostles, and the first of them all, Peter, evinces some disquietude, if not at their lot in this world, at least at their destinies in the kingdom of heaven. "Then answered Peter and said unto him, Behold, we have forsaken all, and followed thee; what shall we have therefore? And Jesus said unto them, Verily I say unto you, That ye which have followed me, in the regeneration when the Son of man shall sit in the throne of his glory, ye also shall sit upon twelve thrones, judging the twelve tribes of Israel. And every one that hath forsaken houses, or brethren, or sisters, or father, or mother, or wife, or children, or lands, for my name's sake, shall receive an hundredfold, and shall inherit everlasting life." [Footnote 95]

[Footnote 95: Matthew xix. 27-29.]

But Jesus does not intend that the prospect of their lofty inheritance should inspire in the minds of any of his apostles, and not more in that of Peter than the rest, any proud presumptuousness, and He immediately adds, "But many that are first, shall be last; and the last shall be first." [Footnote 96]

[Footnote 96: Matthew xix. 30.]

The world's history may be perused and reperused; the causes of all the revolutions that have taken place in the world, whether religious or political, may be probed and investigated; but we shall nowhere be able to trace in the dealings of chiefs and accomplices, of originators and fellow-workmen, the divine characteristics of absolute and uncompromising sincerity that reign throughout the actions and language of Jesus Christ in His conduct towards His apostles. Them He has chosen and loved; to them He has entrusted His work; but He practises with them no arts of worldly wisdom; He withholds nothing from them; here is no faltering encouragement, no exaggeration in the promises that He makes or in the hope that He holds forth; He speaks to them the language of pure truth, and it is in the name of that truth that He gives them His commands and transfers to them His mission. "Never did man speak like this man," [Footnote 97] nor so deal with men.

[Footnote 97: John vii. 46.]

II. Jesus Christ And His Precepts.

Jesus speaks:—and it is at one time with His disciples alone, at another surrounded by eager, astonished multitudes; now from the mount, now on the shore of the sea of Gennesareth, from a bark; by the road side; in the house of the Pharisee, Simon, and the toll-gatherer, Levi; in the synagogue of Nazareth, in the Temple of Jerusalem:—Jesus speaks, "not like the scribes," not like the philosophers; He expounds no system; He discusses no question; He does not pace up and down like Socrates with his learned friends in the gardens of the Academy, nor lose himself in the mazes of the human understanding. Jesus speaks to men, to all men without distinction; He speaks to them of man's life, man's soul, man's destiny, of matters that touch all alike. And He speaks to them "as one having authority."

What does He say to them? What teach, what command, in that speech full of authority?

He teaches them, He enjoins them, to have faith, hope, charity: those virtues which have now borne His name nineteen centuries, those virtues which are essentially Christian.

Is it, then, in His own name that Jesus Christ teaches and commands? By no means: "My doctrine is not mine, but his that sent me. If any man will do his will, he shall know of the doctrine, whether it be of God, or whether I speak of myself.

"He that speaketh of himself seeketh his own glory: but he that seeketh his glory that sent him, the same is true, and no unrighteousness is in him. ... Then cried Jesus in the Temple as he taught, saying, Ye both know me, and ye know whence I am: I am not come of myself, but he that sent me is true, whom ye know not.

"But I know him: for I am from him, and he hath sent me." [Footnote 98]

[Footnote 98: John vii. 16-18, 28, 29.]

Whilst He refers everything to God, Jesus Christ seeks not to define or explain Him; He affirms Him and demonstrates Him; God is the first cause, the point from which all things spring; faith in God is the paramount source of virtue, and of power, as well as virtue, of hope and of resignation.

For Jesus Christ has not only a perfect faith in God, He has also a profound knowledge of man: He knows that, unaided, man's soul cannot, with out despair, without withering, bear the burthen imposed by the injustice of the world and of life, of the miseries and erroneous appreciation of mankind. To this injustice and this wretchedness Jesus Christ never ceases to oppose God, God's justice, God's benevolence, God's succour: He recommends to Him all the forsaken, all the oppressed, all the wretched, all the victims of society. He enjoins to these not resignation alone, but Hope as the sister and companion of Faith. Nor does He hold forth to those that suffer the realization of earthly expectations, the restoration of worldly prosperity, as their resource and their consolation. He has nothing to do with remedies deceitful like these. He acts with the most perfect truthfulness and sincerity towards mankind in general, as He also does with His disciples: He only promises them the re-establishment of justice, and the reward of virtue, in that mysterious future where God alone reigns, and of which He discloses to them the perspective without unfolding the secrets.

Nothing strikes me more in the Gospel than this double character of austerity and of love, of severe purity and tender sympathy, which constantly appears, which reigns in the actions and the words of Jesus Christ in everything that touches the relation of God and mankind. To Jesus Christ the law of God is absolute, sacred; the violation of the law, and sin, are odious to Him; but the sinner himself irresistibly moves him and attracts him: "What man of you, having an hundred sheep, if he lose one of them, doth not leave the ninety and nine in the wilderness, and go after that which is lost, until he find it? And when he hath found it, he layeth it on his shoulders, rejoicing. And when he cometh home, he calleth together his friends and neighbours, saying unto them, Rejoice with me; for I have found my sheep which was lost. I say unto you, that likewise joy shall be in heaven over one sinner that repenteth, more than over ninety and nine just persons, which need no repentance." [Footnote 99]

[Footnote 99: Luke xv. 4-7.]

Jesus said unto them, "They that are whole need not a physician, but they that are sick. ... For I am not come to call the righteous, but sinners to repentance." [Footnote 100]

[Footnote 100: Matthew ix. 12, 13.]

What is the signification of this sublime fact; what the meaning in Jesus of this union, this harmony of severity and of love, of saint-like holiness and of human sympathy? It is Heaven's revelation of the nature of Jesus him-self, of the God-man. God, he made himself man. God is his father, men are his brethren. He is pure and holy like God: He is accessible and sensible to all that man feels. Thus the vital principles of the Christian faith, the divine and the human nature united in Jesus, start to evidence, in his sentiments and language respecting the relations between God and man. The dogma is the foundation of the principles.

Another fact is not less significant. At the same time that the divine and mysterious character of Jesus Christ appears in the Gospel, his acts and his words have a character essentially simple and practical. He pursues no learned object, no scientific plan; He develops no system; his object is something infinitely grander than the triumph of any logical abstraction: it is to pervade the human soul, to establish himself in it—to save it. He speaks the language—He appeals to the ideas most calculated to ensure Him success. Sometimes He addresses himself to the task of inspiring in men the most poignant disquietude as to their future destiny, if they violate the laws of God; at other times He causes to shine before their eyes the realisation of the most magnificent hopes, if with sincerity they persist in faith. He knows the generation that He is addressing; He knows human nature in its universality, and what it will be in future generations: his object is to produce upon it an effect at once positive, general, durable; He chooses the ideas, He employs the images suitable to his design for the regeneration and the salvation of all. God's Ambassador is the most penetrating and able of human moralists.

More than once, the attempt has been made to find Him at fault, to detect in his language exaggerations, contradictions, incoherencies irreconcilable with his divine authority. Surprise, for instance, has been expressed, that He should have one day said, according to St. Matthew: "He that is not with me is against me; and he that gathereth not with me scattereth abroad;" [Footnote 101] and that He should another day, according to St. Mark, have used the expression, "For he that is not against us is on our part." [Footnote 102]

[Footnote 101: Matthew xii. 30.]

[Footnote 102: Mark ix. 40.]

These two passages have been characterised as furnishing "two rules of proselytism entirely opposed to each other, and as involving a contradiction growing out of some impassioned struggle." [Footnote 103]

[Footnote 103: Vie de Jesus, par M. Renan, p. 229.]

In my turn I observe that it astonishes me how earnest men can fall into any such error. Jesus does not lay down in these two passages two contradictory rules of proselytism, He merely observes and refers in turn to two different facts: who has not learnt, in the course of actual life, that, according to the difference of circumstances and persons, the man who abstains from active concurrence, who keeps himself aloof, by that very fact may at one time give support and strength, and at another injure and impede? These two assertions, far from being in contradiction, may be both true, and Jesus Christ, in uttering them, spoke as a sagacious observer, not as a moralist who is enunciating precepts. I have heard other critics reproachfully regard another passage as a sort of blasphemy. According to St Luke: "There was in a city a judge, which feared not God, neither regarded man: and there was a widow in that city; and she came unto him, saying, Avenge me of mine adversary. And he would not for a while: but afterward he said within himself, Though I fear not God, nor regard man; yet because this widow troubleth me, I will avenge her, lest by her continual coming she weary me." [Footnote 104]

[Footnote 104: Luke xviii. 1-5.]

Is it possible to infer from these words an intention on the part of Jesus to liken God to an unjust judge, and to make the mere importunate persistence in praying a claim to God's grace? He only cited an occurrence which made noise in his time, in order to instil a lively impression of the utility of perseverance. To attain his end, He never makes use of out-of-the-way or impure expedients; but He draws from the ordinary events of human life examples and reasons to illustrate and render intelligible the divine precepts, and to insure their acceptance. All the parables have this meaning and object.

Next to the precepts which refer to the relations of man with God come those which respect the relations of men with one another. Whilst Faith and Hope regard God, Charity has man for its object.

Charity, it has often been repeated, is the great principle of Jesus Christ, pre-eminently the Christian virtue. I know, not, however, whether the source whence Christian charity derives its character and grandeur has been adequately perceived or remarked.

In the different pagan religions, whether of character gross or learned, we have deifications of the different forces of nature or of men themselves. And even in those religions in which gods in their turn are said to assume man's shape, it is man particularly that is predominant, and that lives in the incarnation of God. Whereas in Christianity, it is not a god sprung from nature or of human origin that becomes man, but the God self-existent, anterior, and superior to all beings, the God, One, Eternal. The Hebrew religion, alone of all religions, shows God essentially and eternally distinct from the nature and the mankind that He has created, and that He governs. The Christian Faith alone shows God one and eternal; the God of Abraham and of Moses making himself man, and the divine nature uniting itself to the human nature in the person of Jesus. And in this union it is the divine nature that shines forth, that speaks, that sets in movement. And this incarnation is unparalleled like the God its author.

And why did God make himself man? "What is the object of this unparalleled, this mysterious incarnation? It is God's purpose to rescue man from the evil and the peril which have continued to weigh upon him since the fault committed by his first progenitor. It is God's purpose to ransom the human race from the sin of Adam, the heritage of Adam's children, and to bring it back to the ways of eternal life. These are the designs, loudly proclaimed, of the divine incarnation in Jesus, and the price of all the sufferings and agonies which He endured in its accomplishment.

Need I say more? Who does not see how this sublime fact exalts man's dignity at the same time that it illustrates the worth of man's nature? By the mere fact of God having assumed his form is man's nature glorified; and all men, so to say, have their share of the honour done by God to humanity in uniting himself with it, and in accepting, for a moment of time, all the conditions of humanity. But as far as mankind is here concerned, it is far more than a mere accession of an honour or a glorifying of his nature: it is a striking manifestation of the value that all men have in the eyes of God. For it is not for some of them only, for some class or nation, or portion of humanity, it is for all humanity that God became incarnate in Jesus Christ, and that Jesus Christ has submitted to all human sufferings. Every human soul is the object of this divine sacrifice, and called upon to gather the fruit.

This is the source, this the privilege of Christian charity. The dogma makes the force of the precept itself. Jesus crucified is God's charity towards man. Impossible that men should not feel themselves bound to act towards each other as God has done to them; and towards what man is not charity a duty? Without the divinity and sacrifice of Jesus Christ, the value of man's soul, if I may be pardoned the expression, sinks,—neither his salvation nor the example of his Saviour is any longer the question,—charity becomes nothing more than human goodness; a sentiment, however noble and useful, still limited both in impulsive energy and in efficacy; having its source in man alone, it can but incompletely solace the unequally distributed sufferings of mortality. It is not suited to inspire any long effort or great sacrifice: it is not adequate to convert the longing desire for the moral amendment, the physical relief of humanity, into that inextinguishable sympathy and untiring and impassioned emotion which really constitute charity, and which the Christian Faith, in the history of the world, has alone been able to inspire.

Thus the essential precepts of Jesus, the virtues which He commands as the basis and source of all the others, have an intimate connection with his doctrine, a doctrine "which is not," He tells us himself, "***his***, but of him that sent him;" that is to say, they are connected with the fundamental dogmas of the Christian religion. No one denies the perfection, the sublimity of the Gospel morality; men indeed seem to feel a sort of self-complacency, a satisfaction in celebrating it, with a view to the conclusion, more or less explicitly stated, that that morality constitutes the whole Gospel. This is, however, not less than absolutely to mistake the bond which unites in man thought with sentiment, and belief with action. Man is grander and less easy to satisfy than superficial moralists pretend; the law of his life is for him, in the profound instinct of his soul, necessarily connected with the secret of his destiny; and it is only the Christian dogma that gives to Christian ethics the Royal authority of which they stand in need to govern and to regenerate humanity.

III. Jesus And His Miracles.

I have called myself one of those who admit the supernatural; and I have stated my reasons. I might stop there and enter into no special reflection as to the Gospel Miracles. The possibility of miracles once accorded in principle, nothing remains but to weigh the value of the testimony in their support. In the second series of these ***Meditations***, where I treat of the authenticity of the localities specified in the Holy Scriptures, I shall occupy myself with this examination. It is not, however, my wish to elude, upon the subjects that lie at the bottom of this question, any of the difficulties that it presents: for here we find the point of attack sought by the adversaries of the Christian faith. The image of Christ as it results from the Gospel would be besides singularly unfaithful, did we not range in it his miracles by the side of his precepts.

I avow once more my belief in God, in God the Creator, the Sovereign Master of the Universe, who orders it and governs it by that independent and constant action of his providence and power styled the Laws of Nature. To those who regard nature as having existed from all eternity of itself, and governed by laws immutable and proceeding from fate, I have nothing to say of Jesus or his miracles; the question at issue between them and me is more important than that which respects miracles; it involves the very question of Pantheism or Christianity, of Fatalism or Liberty, affecting both God and man. Upon these subjects I have already expressed my general opinion and its grounds. I propose to enter further upon it in the third series of these ***Meditations***, when I come to speak of the different systems which are now in conflict throughout Christendom. But at this moment I address myself to Deists and to men of wavering minds, and to these alone.

One thing is beyond all doubt: the perfect sincerity of the apostles and of the primitive Christians as to their faith in the miracles of Jesus. Sincerity still more striking that it is united to every sort of hesitation in the mind and weakness in the conduct, and that it only triumphs gradually and slowly when Jesus has quitted his disciples and has left them alone charged with his work. Whilst He was with them, St. Peter has failed, St. Thomas has doubted; after several miracles have been performed by Jesus, his disciples are astonished, put questions to Him, yet still doubt of Him and of his power. Upon several occasions Jesus addresses them as men "of little faith," and at the moment when He is arrested, they abandon Him, they fly from Him. No impassioned enthusiasm, no exaggeration in their trustfulness and their devotedness; even with them Jesus sees himself confronted by all the vacillations and pusillanimity of humanity; He persuades them, He wins them, He preserves them only by great exertion, and by dint, so to say, of divine power and divine virtue. They only really believe in Him after having witnessed the accomplishment of his sacrifice and his last miracle, when they had seen his Crucifixion and his Resurrection. Only then they believed; but from that moment their faith became absolute, superior to all perils and all trials: full of the Holy Spirit, and associated in a certain measure to their divine Master, they pursue his work with unshaken confidence and firmness, without pretending to any merit, without any impulse of personal pride. Before "the gate of the Temple which is called Beautiful," St. Peter has healed a lame man and made him to walk. "And as the lame man which was healed held Peter and John, all the people ran together unto them in the porch that is called Solomon's, greatly wondering. And when Peter saw it, he answered unto the people, Ye men of Israel, why marvel ye at this? or why look ye so earnestly on us, as though by our own power or holiness we had made this man to walk? ... Ye killed the Prince of life, whom God hath raised from the dead; whereof we are witnesses. And his name through faith in his name hath made this man strong, whom ye see and know: yea, the faith which is by him hath given him this perfect soundness in the presence of you all." [Footnote 105]

[Footnote 105: Acts iii. 1-16.]

It was not the people only that felt astonishment, but "the rulers and elders; the scribes, the high priest, and all those who were of the kindred of the high priest, were gathered together at Jerusalem, and set in their midst "Peter and John, and after a deliberation full of anxiety, they "commanded them not to speak at all, nor teach in the name of Jesus. But Peter and John answered and said unto them, Whether it be right in the sight of God to hearken unto you more than unto God, judge ye. For we cannot but speak the things we have seen and heard." [Footnote 106]

[Footnote 106: Acts iv. 5, 6, 18-20.]

What sincerity and what firmness ever showed themselves more strikingly than those that grew out of the faith of St. Paul? From such faith he had been originally farther removed than the other apostles; he had done far more than merely err like Peter or doubt like Thomas; he had hotly persecuted the first followers of Christ. In his turn penetrated and subdued on the road to Damascus by the voice of Jesus, he devotes himself to Him life and soul; he recounts himself his miraculous conversion, [Footnote 107] and as little doubt can be entertained of the authenticity of his Epistles as of the sincerity that dictated them.

[Footnote 107: 1 Corinthians xv. 8. 2 Corinthians xi. 32, 33; xii. 1-5. Galatians i. 1-4.]

The history of all religions abounds in miracles; but in all religions except the Christian, the miracles recounted by their historians are evidently either contrivances of the founder to induce persuasion, or they spring from the play of the human imagination, ever disposed to delight in the marvellous, ever particularly prone to give way in the sphere of religion to its fantastic suggestions. In the Gospel miracles, on the contrary, we have nothing of the kind; no artifice in their Author; none of the marvellous machinery of poetry, nor any hasty credulity in the historians. The miraculous agency of Christ is essentially simple, practical, and moral: He does not go in search of miracles; neither does He make any vain display of them: they are wrought when a pressing emergency or a natural occasion calls for them; and when they are demanded in faith and in trust, He then works them without ostentation and in right of his divine mission; whilst at the very moment He makes the doubt and the coldness with which He is received, the subject of complaint: "Woe unto thee, Chorazin! wo unto thee, Bethsaida! for if the mighty works, which were done in you, had been done in Tyre and Sidon, they would have repented long ago in sackcloth and ashes." [Footnote 108] Jesus has full confidence in himself, in the miracles that He effects, in the doctrine that He inculcates. He feels no astonishment, but merely sorrow, that His work, the work of light and of salvation, pursued by Him in accordance with the will of God his Father, should not obtain a more rapid, a more general success.

[Footnote 108: Matthew xi. 21.]

As for us, remote spectators, the astonishment must be not the slowness or limited nature of that success, but its rapidity and its extent. All religions that have taken place in the world's history, have been established by moral and by material agency; all appealed from their very commencement as much to force as to persuasion, as much to the arm as to the tongue. Christianity alone lived and grew during three centuries by its own single native virtue, without any other appeal than that made to Truth, without any other aid than that of Faith. During those three centuries the dogmas, the precepts, and the miracles of its Author constituted its only weapons, and weapons which have prevailed against all other arms. Those dogmas, those precepts, and those miracles effected the conquest of man's mind and of human society in spite of the resistance of Greek philosophy, Roman power, and all the poetical or mystical mythologies of antiquity marshalled against them. The victory has not, it is true, put an end to all struggle of man's intelligence: neither has the light from Christ dissipated all darkness, nor satisfied all minds; the explanation and commentaries of man have obscured the doctrines of Christ; human prejudices have mistaken his precepts; and legends have been grafted upon his miracles. But the fact does not the less exist, that the dogmas, the precepts, and the miracles of Christ, without any aid from human sources, sufficed to found and ensure the triumph of the Christian religion: this is a fact primitive and supreme. And from this single result shines forth the divine character of the Christian religion, for its triumph without the miraculous agency of God, would be of all miracles the most impossible to receive.

IV. Jesus, The Jews, And The Gentiles.

Think not that I am come to destroy the law, or the prophets: I am not come to destroy, but to fulfil." [Footnote 109]

[Footnote 109: Matthew v. 17.]

"Do not think that I will accuse you to the Father: there is one that accuseth you, even Moses, in whom ye trust. For had ye believed Moses, ye would have believed me: for he wrote of me. But if ye believe not his writings, how shall ye believe my words?" [Footnote 110]

[Footnote 110: John v. 45-47.]

This was the language that Jesus used to the Jews. It was in the name of their history and of their faith, in the name of the God of Abraham and of Jacob, that He called them to Him, presenting himself to them in the double capacity of conservative and reformer, and appealing to the ancient law against those who, whilst observing it outwardly, really changed its character. "Then came to Jesus scribes and Pharisees, which were of Jerusalem, saying, Why do thy disciples transgress the tradition of the elders? for they wash not their hands when they eat bread. But He answered and said unto them, "Why do ye also transgress the commandment of God by your tradition? For God commanded, saying, Honour thy father and mother: and, He that curseth father or mother, let him die the death. But ye say, Whosoever shall say to his father or his mother, It is a gift, by whatsoever thou mightest be profited by me; and honour not his father or his mother, he shall be free. Thus ye have made the commandment of God of none effect by your tradition![Footnote 111] … Woe unto you, scribes and Pharisees, hypocrites! for ye pay tithe of mint and anise and cummin, and have omitted the weightier matters of the law, judgment, mercy, and faith: these ought ye to have done, and not to leave the other undone." [Footnote 112]

[Footnote 111: Matthew xv. 1-6.]

[Footnote 112: Matthew xxiii. 23.]

Jesus was incessantly warning, making appeals to the Jews; and when He saw that they pertinaciously disavowed and rejected Him, He cried, in an impulse of patriotic, affectionate sadness:—"O Jerusalem, Jerusalem, which killest the prophets, and stonest them that are sent unto thee; how often would I have gathered thy children together, as a hen doth gather her brood under her wings, and ye would not!" [Footnote 113]

[Footnote 113: Matthew xxiii. 37. Luke xiii. 34.]

I know nothing more imposing than the apparition of a grand idea, a divine idea rising and mounting rapidly upon the human horizon. Such is the spectacle afforded to us in its short duration by the history of Jesus Christ. In his first instructions to his apostles, He said to them, "Go not to the Gentiles and enter not into any city of the Samaritans; but go ye rather to the lost sheep of the people of Israel." Thus he carefully avoided offending the sentiments of the day, and only enjoined upon his apostles what they might do with success at the very beginning of their mission. But soon the light increases that issues from the words and the actions of Jesus; as I advance in the books of the Gospel, I there read: "And when Jesus was entered into Capernaum, there came unto him a centurion, beseeching him, and saying, Lord, my servant lieth at home sick of the palsy, grievously tormented. And Jesus saith unto him, I will come and heal him. The centurion answered and said, Lord, I am not worthy that thou shouldest come under my roof: but speak the word only, and my servant shall be healed. For I am a man under authority, having soldiers under me: and I say to this man, Go, and he goeth; and to another, Come, and he cometh; and to my servant, Do this, and he doeth it. When Jesus heard it, he marvelled, and said to them that followed, Verily I say unto you, I have not found so great faith, no, not in Israel. And I say unto you, That many shall come from the east and west, and shall sit down with Abraham, and Isaac, and Jacob, in the kingdom of heaven." [Footnote 114]

[Footnote 114: Matthew viii. 5-11.]

Thus a great stride has been made; it is no longer for the sheep of the house of Israel that Jesus has come; from the East and from the West will men come to Him, and He will receive them all. To continue the Gospel narrative: departing from the borders of the lake of Gennesareth, Jesus "departed into the coasts of Tyre and Sidon. And, behold, a woman of Canaan came out of the same coasts, and cried unto him, saying, Have mercy on me, O Lord, thou son of David; my daughter is grievously vexed with a devil. But he answered her not a word. And his disciples came and besought him, saying, Send her away; for she crieth after us. But he answered and said, I am not sent but unto the lost sheep of the house of Israel. Then came she and worshipped him, saying, Lord, help me. But he answered and said, It is not meet to take the children's bread, and to cast it to dogs. And she said, Truth, Lord: yet the dogs eat of the crumbs which fall from their master's table. Then Jesus answered and said unto her, O woman, great is thy faith: be it unto thee even as thou wilt." [Footnote 115]

[Footnote 115: Matthew xv. 21-28.]

Another day, near the city Sychar and the well of Jacob, Jesus conversed with a woman of Samaria, who had come there to draw water:—"The woman saith unto him, Sir, I perceive that thou art a prophet. Our fathers worshipped in this mountain; and ye say, that in Jerusalem is the place where men ought to worship. Jesus saith unto her, Woman, believe me, the hour cometh, when ye shall neither in this mountain, nor yet at Jerusalem, worship the Father. ... But the hour cometh, and now is, when the true worshippers shall worship the Father in spirit and in truth: for the Father seeketh such to worship him. God is a Spirit: and they that worship him must worship him in spirit and in truth." [Footnote 116]

[Footnote 116: John iv. 5-24.]

Thus disappears gradually, in the name of the God of the Jews himself, the exclusive privilege of the Jews to the divine revelation and to divine grace. And thus, too, the restricted religion of Israel gives place to the grand catholicity of the religion of Christ. The benefit of the true faith and of salvation is no longer limited to one people, whether great or small, ancient or modern; but is imparted to all the races of mankind. "Go ye therefore, and teach all nations, baptizing them in the name of the Father, and of the Son, and of the Holy Ghost." [Footnote 117] "And he said unto them, Go ye into all the world, and preach the gospel to every creature."[Footnote 118]

[Footnote 117: Matthew xxviii. 19.]

[Footnote 118: Mark xvi. 15.]

These were the last words which Christ addressed to his apostles, and the apostles execute faithfully the instructions of their divine Master; they go forth in effect, preaching in all places and to all nations his history, his doctrine, his precepts, and his parables. St. Paul is the special apostle of the

Gentiles. From Jesus, says this apostle, "We have received grace and apostleship, for obedience to the faith among all nations, for his name." "Is he the God of the Jews only? is he not also of the Gentiles? Yes, of the Gentiles also." "For there is no difference between the Jew and the Greek: for the same Lord over all is rich unto all that call upon him." [Footnote 119]

[Footnote 119: Romans i. 5.; iii. 29; x. 12.]

In spite of his prejudices as a Jew, and of the differences that took place in the infancy of the Church, St. Peter adheres to St. Paul; the apostles and the elders assembled at Jerusalem adhere to St. Peter and St. Paul. The God of Abraham and of Jacob is now not merely the One God, He is the God of the whole human race; to all men alike He prescribes the same faith, the same law, and promises the same salvation.

Another question, more temporal in its nature, still a great, a delicate one, is raised in the presence of Jesus Christ. He withdraws from the Jews their exclusive privilege to the knowledge and the grace of the true God; but what does He think of that which touches their existence as a nation, and as a great one? Does He direct them to rebel and to struggle against their earthly governor and sovereign?—"Then went the Pharisees, and took counsel how they might entangle him in his talk. And they sent out unto him their disciples with the Herodians, saying, Master, we know that thou art true, and teachest the way of God in truth, neither carest thou for any man: for thou regardest not the person of men. Tell us therefore, What thinkest thou? Is it lawful to give tribute unto Cesar, or not? But Jesus perceived their wickedness, and said, Why tempt ye me, ye hypocrites? Shew me the tribute money. And they brought unto him a penny. And he saith unto them, Whose is this image and superscription? They say unto him, Cesar's. Then saith he unto them, Render therefore unto Cesar the things which are Cesar's; and unto God the things that are God's. When they had heard these words, they marvelled, and left him, and went their way." [Footnote 120]

[Footnote 120: Matthew xxii. 15-22. Mark xii. 12-17. Luke xx. 19-25.]

In this reply of Christ there was much more matter for admiration than the Pharisees supposed; it was in effect much more than an adroit evasion of the snare that had been extended for Him; it defined in principle the distinction of man's life as it regards religion, and man's life as it concerns society; the bounds, in fact, of Church and of State. Cæsar has no right to intervene, with his laws and material force, between the soul of man and his God; and on his side, the faithful worshipper of God is bound to fulfil towards Cæsar the duties which the necessity of the maintenance of civil order imposes. The independence of religious faith, and at the same time its subjection to the laws of society, are alike the sense of Christ's reply to the Pharisees, and the divine source of the greatest progress ever made by human society since it began to feel the troubles and agitations of this earth.

I take again these two grand principles, these two great acts of Jesus,—the abolition of every privilege in the relations of God and man, and the distinction of man's religious and his civil life: I confront with these two principles all the history, and every state of society previous to the advent of Jesus Christ, and I am unable to discover in those essentially Christian principles any kindred, any human origin. Everywhere before Christ, religions were national local religions; they were religions which established between nations, classes, individuals, enormous differences and inequalities. Everywhere, also, before Christ, man's civil life and his religious life were confounded, and mutually oppressed each other; that religion or those religions were institutions incorporated in the state, which the state regulated or repressed as its interest dictated. But in this catholicity of religious faith, in this independence of religious communities, I am constrained to recognise new and sublime principles, and to see in them flashes from the light of heaven. It needed many centuries before mental vision was capable of receiving that light; and no one shall pronounce how many centuries will be needed before it will pervade and penetrate the entire world. But whatever difficulties and shortcomings may be reserved in the womb of the future for the two great truths to which I have just referred, it is clear that God caused them first to beam forth from the life and teaching of Jesus Christ.

V. Jesus And Women.

At the very source of all religions, as well as in their subsequent history, women find a place to fill and a part to perform. At one time they constitute the material and furnish the ornament of licentious systems of mythology. At another, on the contrary, they are, for the heroes of those religions, objects either of pious horror or of observances at once rigorous and austere: women are considered by them as creatures full of evil and of peril; and they are accordingly thrust from their lives as men thrust from them what is a temptation and an impurity. Voluptuous pictures and adventures on the one hand, and zealous impulses of rigid asceticism on the other, constitute the two extremes to which religions in their ages of youth and of vigour are alternately prone. Sometimes—and it is more fortunate for women when it is the case—they are described in the narrative of these religions, such as they really are in human life, charmers and at the same time charmed, seducers and seduced, idols and slaves; at first votaries of the enthusiasm, the victims of the errors and the passions which they at once inspire and feel. Whether Asiatic or European, rude or refined, such are the striking features with which all systems of religion, excepting Christianity, have characterised the women whom they have introduced in their narratives.

Neither of these characteristics, nor anything analogous, is met with in the Gospel and in the relations of Jesus with women. They seem irresistibly attracted towards Him, with hearts moved, imaginations struck by his manner of life, his precepts, his miracles, his language. He inspires them with feelings of tender respect and confiding admiration. The Canaanitish woman comes and addresses to Him a timid prayer for the healing of her daughter. The woman of Samaria listens to Him with eagerness, though she does not know Him: Mary seats herself at his feet, absorbed in reflections suggested by his words; and Martha proffers to Him the frank complaint that her sister assists her not, but leaves her unaided in the performance of her domestic duties. The sinner draws near to Him in tears, pouring upon his feet a rare perfume, and wiping them with her hair. The adulteress, hurried into his presence by those who wished to stone her in accordance with the precepts of the Mosaic Law, remains motionless in his presence, even after her accusers have withdrawn, waiting in silence what He is about to say. Jesus receives the homage, and listens to the prayers of all these women, with the gentle gravity and impartial sympathy of a being superior and strange to earthly passion. Pure and inflexible interpreter of the Divine law, He knows and understands man's nature, and judges it with that equitable severity which nothing escapes, the excuse as little as the fault. Faith, sincerity, humanity, sorrow, repentance, touch Him without biassing the charity and the justice of his conclusions; and He expresses blame or announces pardon with the same calm serenity of authority, certain that his eye has read the depths of the heart to which his words will penetrate. In his relations with the women who approach Him, there is, in short, not the slightest trace of man; nowhere does the Godhead manifest itself more winningly and with greater purity. And when there is no longer any question of these particular relations and conversations, when Jesus has no longer before him women suppliants and sinners, who are invoking his power or imploring his clemency; when it is with the position and the destiny of women in general that He is occupying himself, He affirms and defends their claims and their dignity with a sympathy at once penetrating and severe. He knows that the happiness of mankind, as well as the moral position of women, depends essentially upon the married state; He makes of the sanctity of marriage a fundamental law of Christian religion and society; He pursues adultery even into the recesses of the human heart, the human thought; He forbids divorce; He says of men, "Have ye not read, that he which made them at the beginning made them male and female? ... For this cause shall a man leave father and mother, and shall cleave to his wife: and they twain shall be one flesh. Wherefore they are no more twain, but one flesh. What therefore God hath joined together, let not man put asunder. They say unto him, Why did Moses then command to give a writing of divorcement, and to put her away? He saith unto them, Moses because of the hardness of your hearts suffered you to put away your wives: but from the beginning it was not so. And I say unto you, Whosoever shall put away his wife, except it be for fornication, and shall marry another, committeth adultery: and whoso marrieth her which is put away doth commit adultery." [Footnote 121]

> [Footnote 121: Matthew xix. 4-9; v. 27, 28 Mark x. 2-12. Romans vii. 2, 3. 1 Corinthians vi. 16-18; vii. 1-11.]

Signal and striking testimony to the progressive action of God upon the human race! Jesus Christ restores to the divine law of marriage the purity and the authority that Moses had not enjoined to the Hebrews "because of the hardness of their hearts."

VI. Jesus Christ And Children.

The sentiments expressed by Jesus Christ towards children, and the language that He uses towards them, as these appear in the Gospel narrative, must strike even the most careless reader. Let me refer to the passages themselves:—

> "And they brought young children to him, that he should touch them: and his disciples rebuked those that brought them. But when Jesus saw it, he was much displeased, and said unto them, Suffer the little children to come unto me, and forbid them not: for of such is the kingdom of God. Verily I say unto you, Whosoever shall not receive the kingdom of God as a little child, he shall not enter therein. And he took them up in his arms, put his hands upon them, and blessed them." [Footnote 122]
>
> [Footnote 122: Mark x. 13-16; Matthew xix. 13-15. Luke xviii. 15-17.]

Another day, "came the disciples unto Jesus, saying, Who is the greatest in the kingdom of heaven? And Jesus called a little child unto him, and set him in the midst of them, and said, Verily I say unto you, Except ye be converted, and become as little children, ye shall not enter into the kingdom of heaven. Whosoever therefore shall humble himself as this little child, the same is greatest in the kingdom of heaven." [Footnote 123]

[Footnote 123: Matthew xviii. 1-4; Mark ix. 33-37.]

Again another day, Jesus, deploring the coldness that his preaching and his miracles frequently encountered, and that even in his closest vicinity, exclaimed, here no longer addressing his disciples, but God himself, "I thank thee, O Father, Lord of heaven and earth, because thou hast hid these things from the wise and prudent, and hast revealed them unto babes." [Footnote 124]

[Footnote 124: Matthew xi. 25.]

What is the full meaning of these words? They are not simply the expression of that impulse of gentle benevolence excited in all hearts at the sight of children, and their innocent confidence in all who come near them. Jesus Christ no doubt experienced the influence of this feeling, for He was strange to none of man's noble emotions; but his thoughts passed far beyond the children whose approach he permitted, and they merely furnished Him with the living occasion to address to men themselves his solemn warnings.

The child, I have already mentioned in these Meditations,[Footnote 125] is, for us, the image of innocence, the type of the creature fallible, yet who has not yet sinned, who knows not yet either error of understanding, or the seduction of passion, or the blinding influence of pride, or the troubles of doubt, or the extreme folly of sin, or the anguish of repentance; who follows in the first impulses of infancy only the spontaneous instincts of tender confidence in the parent to whom he is indebted for security and for love, for the first joys and the earliest blessings.

[Footnote 125: Meditation II., Christian Dogmas, p. 48.]

Jesus does not pretend to bring men back to that fair condition, to restore to them their primitive innocence: but He comes to ransom them from sin; He brings them the hope of pardon and salvation. Confidence in God, a confidence sincere, unpretending, and loving, is that disposition which opens the soul of man to the divine blessing. This is also the disposition that the child evinces towards its parents; he calls upon them, and he hopes in them.

Hence those words of Jesus: "Suffer little children to come unto me, and forbid them not, for of such is the kingdom of heaven." The way of innocence is a far better way than that of science to lead man up to God.

Science is a splendid thing; it is also a noble privilege of man that God, in creating him an intelligent and a free agent, has given him a capacity to desire and to pursue through study the truths of science, and even to attain them in a certain measure, and in a certain sphere. But when science attempts to exceed that measure and to quit that sphere; when it ignores and scorns the instincts,—natural, universal, and permanent instincts, of the human soul; when it essays to set up everywhere its own torch in the place of that primitive light that lights mankind: then, and from that cause alone, science fills itself with error; and this is the very case which called forth those words of Jesus: "I praise thee, Father, Lord of heaven and of earth, that thou hast hidden these things from the wise and prudent, and hast revealed them unto babes." [Footnote 126]

> [Footnote 126: Matthew xi. 25. The words ἀπὸ σοφῶν καὶ συνετῶν are better rendered, "from the learned and the prudent," than "wise and intelligent;" "sages et intelligents," as in the French version by Osterwald.]

VII. Jesus Christ Himself.

I have sought to gather from the Gospels the scattered facts that constitute the life of Jesus. I have searched for them in his acts, his precepts, his words: in his different relations in life. I have added nothing, exaggerated nothing; on the contrary, the life of Jesus is infinitely grander and more sublime than I have made it; his words are infinitely more profound and admiral than I have described them. And I have said nothing of the seal affixed to ***his work*** and ***his mission*** by his Passion; nor have I shown Jesus at Gethsemane and upon the Cross.

According to the Bible, God is without parallel—ever the same. Jesus is also so according to the Gospel. The most perfect, the most constant unity reigns in Him: in his life as in his soul; in his language as in his acts. His action is progressive, and proportionate to the circumstances which call it forth and in the midst of which He lives; but his progress never entails any change of character or purpose. As He appears at the age of twelve, in the Temple, already full of the sentiment of his divine nature, in his reply to his mother who was searching for Him with disquietude, "Knowest thou not that I must be about my Father's business?" the same He remains and manifests himself in the whole course of his active mission—in Galilee and at Jerusalem, with his apostles and with the people, amongst the Pharisees and the Publicans, whether they be men, or women, or children who approach Him; alike before Caiaphas and Pilate, and under the eyes of the crowd pressing around to listen to Him. Everywhere and in every circumstance, the same spirit animates Him; He diffuses the same light, proclaims the same law. Perfect and immutable, always at once Son of God and Son of Man, He pursues and consummates amidst all the trials and all the sorrows of human existence his divine work for the salvation of mankind.

What need to add more? How speak in detail of Jesus himself when one believes in Him, when one sees in Him God made man, acting as God alone can act, and suffering all that man can suffer to ransom mankind from sin, and save it by bringing it back to God? How sound closely the mysteries of such a person and such a purpose? What passed in that divine soul during that human existence? Who shall explain those cries of agony of Jesus in the bosom of the most absolute faith in God his father and in himself, and those moments of horror at the approach of the sacrifice without the slightest hesitation in the sacrifice, without the smallest doubt as to its efficaciousness? This sublime fact, this intimate and continual intermixture of the divine and human finds no competent, no adequate expression in human speech, and the more we consider it the more difficult we find it to speak of it.

Those who have no faith in Jesus, who admit not the supernatural character of his person, of his life, and of his work, do not feel this difficulty. Having beforehand done away with God and with miracles, the history of Jesus is for them nothing more than an ordinary history, which they narrate and explain like any other biography of man. But such historians fall into a far different difficulty, and wreck themselves on a far different rock. The supernatural being and power of Jesus may be disputed, but the perfection, the sublimity of his actions and of his precepts, of his life and of his moral law, are incontestable. And in effect, not only are they not contested, but they are admired and celebrated enthusiastically, and complacently, too; it would seem as if it were desired to restore to Jesus as man, and man alone, the superiority of which men deprive Him in refusing to see in Him the Godhead. But then, what incoherence, what contradictions, what falsehood, what moral impossibility in his history, such as they make it; what a series of suppositions, irreconcilable with fact, nevertheless admitted! The man they make so perfect, so sublime, becomes by turns a dreamer or a charlatan; at once dupe and deceiver: dupe of his own mystical enthusiasm in believing in his own miracles; deceiver in tampering with evidence in order to accredit himself. The history of Jesus Christ is thus but a tissue of fables and falsehood. And nevertheless the hero of this history remains perfect, sublime, incomparable; the greatest genius, the noblest heart that the world ever saw; the type of virtue and moral beauty, the supreme and rightful chief of mankind. And his disciples, in their turn justly admirable, have braved everything, suffered everything, in order to abide faithful to Him and to accomplish his work. And, in effect, the work has been accomplished: the pagan world has become Christian, and the whole world has nothing better to do than to follow the example.

What a contradictory and insolvable problem they present to us instead of the one they are so anxious to suppress!

History reposes upon two foundations—positive written evidence as to facts and persons, and presumptive evidence resulting from the connection of facts and the action of persons. These two foundations are entirely lost sight of in the history of Jesus such as it is recounted, or rather constructed, in these days; it is, on the one hand, in evident and shocking contradiction with the testimony of the men who saw Jesus, or of the men who lived nearly in the time of those who had seen Him; on the other side, with the natural laws presiding over the actions of men and the course of events. This does not deserve the name of historical criticism; it is a philosophical system and a romantic narrative substituted for the substantial proof and the circumstantial evidence; it is a Jesus false and impossible, made by the hand of man pretending to dethrone the real living Jesus—the Son of God.

The choice lies between the system and the mystery; between the romance of man and the purpose of God. Even in revealing himself God still interposes veils, but these veils are no falsehoods. The Gospel history of Jesus shows us God acting in ways which are not his ways of every day. This special action of God characterises also many other facts in the history of the universe; amongst others, the great fact of the actual creation, where man, at his appearance upon earth, received the first divine revelation. The supernatural does not merely date from Jesus Christ; and if a man from this motive rejects the history of Jesus, he will have to deny also a far different thing. To escape this fatal necessity, men of learning have recently striven to curtail indefinitely the proportion of the supernatural in the history of Jesus, and to explain by natural means, most of the acts and circumstances of his life. A puerile attempt, which has altogether failed in the details, still leaving untouched the substance of the problem. No better success will attend the new attempt that has in these days been made, and which consists in placing the Ideal in the place of the Supernatural, and in elevating religious sentiment upon the ruins of the Christian faith. This is doing either too much or too little. The human soul is not satisfied with these leavings, nor human pride with such refusals, When one is so hardy as to pretend, in the name of the science of man in this finite world, to determine the limits of the power of God, one must be still more hardy and—dethrone God himself.

Note.

I said (p. 145) that I would indicate some instances of grammatical faults to be met with in the Scriptures, to which the character of divine inspiration cannot be assigned. Upon the subject of the books of the Old Testament I have consulted my learned confrère, M. Munk; his reply is in the precise words which follow:

> "The biblical authors," he writes to me, "whose style is most incorrect, are Ezekiel and Jeremiah. These authors, and particularly the first, err frequently against grammar and orthography; they are not merely influenced by the Aramean dialect, but they disclose grammatical faults capable of being traced to no source in any of the Semitic dialects. This remark has also been made by Hebrew grammarians of the middle ages, and Isaac Abrabanel (towards the close of the 15th century), in the preface to his commentary upon Ezekiel, does not hesitate to declare that this prophet was but superficially acquainted with Hebrew grammar and orthography. Nevertheless, neither Jeremiah nor Ezekiel, of whom both are distinguished by a certain originality of style, unlike that of any of the other Hebrew writers, is wanting in elegance, energy, and boldness in images, and they display in the highest degree their proficiency in the art of composition. The following are some instances of the grave faults against grammar to be met with in their writings:—

Examples of Incorrect Expressions in Ezekiel.

- והמה משתחויתם (***mischta' hawithem***), "and they worshipped" (viii. 16), a barbarism for משתחוים (***mischta'hawîm***).
- ונאשאר אני (***we-néschaar ani***), "and I remained" (xi. 8), for ואשאר (***wa-ëschaër***) or ונשארתי (***we-nischarti***). (There are here faults both of orthography and grammar.)
- אשת (***ischôth***), "women" (xxiii. 44), for נשי (***nesché***).
- שבעה עולותו (***schib'a***), "his seven burnt offerings" (xl. 26), for שבע (***scheba'***). In the number seven the masculine is used instead of the feminine.
- בבנותיך (***bi-benôthayikh***), "in that thou buildest" (xvi. 31), instead of בבנותך (***bi-benotihékh***).

- בשובני (***be-schoubéni***), "when I returned" (xlvi. 7), instead of בשובי (***be-schoubi***).
- גבהא קמתו (***gabehâ***), "his height was exalted" (xxxi. 5), instead of גבהה (***gabehâ***). The last letter is ***aleph***, for ***hé***.

The Chaldean plural is used in several words, for instance:

- חטין (***'hittîn***), "wheat" (iv. 9), for חטים (***'hittîm***); האין (***ha-iyyîn***), "the isles," or "the isles in the sea" (xxvi. 18), instead of האים ***(ha-iyyim***), an error in both orthography and grammar.

Examples of Incorrect Expressions in Jeremiah.

- אובידה (***ôbîdâ***), "I will destroy" (xlvi. 8), for אאבידה (***aabîdâ***).
- נבית (***nibbĕtha***), "hast thou prophesied" (xxvi. 9), instead of נבאת (***nibbētha***). The syllable ***bé*** has a ***yod*** instead of an ***aleph***.
- אתנו (***athanou***) "we come" (iii. 22), instead of אתינו (***athinou.***).
- אתי (***att***), "thee" in the feminine (terminating with ***yod*** mute), for את (***att***), a Syriasm very frequent in Jeremiah, who often forms the second person of the perfect fem. in תי־ (***t*** followed by ***yod***) instead of ת־ (***t***).
- לוא (***lô*** written with ***waw*** quiescent), "not" very often for לא (***lô*** without the ***waw***).
- הגלת (***hoglath***), "shall be carried away captive" (xiii. 19), instead of הגלתה (***hoglethâ***). The latter Chaldaism we meet also in the Pentateuch (Leviticus xxv. 22), ועשת (***we'asath***), her fruits (shall) come in." for ועשתה (***we'asetah***), and ibid xxvi. 34; והרצת (***we-hirzath***), "she shall enjoy," for והרצתה (***we-hircethâ***).

With respect to the New Testament, I have required a similar notice from my son William, who has made the Greek language in general, and its deviations in the writings of the Gospel, the object of particular and careful study. I insert, also, the note which he has drawn up upon the subject:—

> "On first approaching the text of the New Testament, after having learnt the Greek language and grammar in the classical writers, we are struck by numerous irregularities of expression: amongst these, however, we must carefully distinguish those which constitute merely

particular and singular modes of expression from those which are real faults. The former are susceptible of explanation and justification by different examples and different arguments; the latter are not capable of being reconciled with the elementary and necessary laws of language. Thus we may justify such or such a strange form of conjugation or of declension, which would be accounted a barbarism by a school boy, but which was nevertheless in actual use in some one or other of the local dialects, written and spoken by the Greeks. Again, however it may have been the rule in Greek to set the verb in the singular when used with a neuter substantive in the plural, the rule has not been invariably observed even by the purest classical writers, and we may justify by exceptions collected here and there in their compositions, several passages of the New Testament which, at first sight, might appear amenable to a charge of solecism. Thus, in short, after our attention having, at first sight, been arrested and our minds disconcerted by other passages in which the sacred writer has confounded the sense of two words which resemble each other, as μαρτύρομαι, which signifies ***summon a witness***, and which St. Peter employs instead of μαρτυρέω which means, ***give testimony***,[Footnote 127] as ἀδυνάτειν, which signifies ***to be incapable***, and which St. Matthew and St. Mark employ in the sense of ***being impossible***, [Footnote 128]—as μεσουράνημα, which signifies the ***meridian or zenith of a star***, and which, on three occasions in the New Testament, is used in the sense of ***in the middle of the air***,—or, even when we meet words, not merely strange to the ear, but formed without attention to the rules and in contradiction to analogy, as πειθός for πείθανος[Footnote 129]—we may again, without any departure from logical rules, by judicious or subtle distinctions, escape from the difficulties which the passages suggest, and have a perfect right to do so. But after having made allowances for the irregularities susceptible of explanation in the language of the New Testament, there still remain some which are real faults. The same word cannot be written by the same hand, at an interval of but three pages, both masculine and feminine, as the word ἶρις, ***rainbow***, in the ***Apocalypse***. [Footnote 130] When the substantive is feminine, the adjective cannot be masculine, as τὴν ληνὸν ... τὸν μέγαν. [Footnote 131]

[Footnote 127: 1 Peter i. 11.]

[Footnote 128: Matthew xvii. 20; Luke i. 37.]

[Footnote 129: 1 Corinthians ii 1.]

[Footnote 130: Compare iv. 3, and x. 1.]

[Footnote 131: Apocalypse xiv. 19.]

When the substantive is in the accusative, the adjective cannot be in the nominative. In such an employment of words we are able to trace in the sacred writings the hand of man, marks of human imperfection and error; and we must not forget that these faults become more numerous and grosser the greater the antiquity of the MS. in which we find them, and the purer the Jewish origin of the writer. Thus the Greek of the Apocalypse is singularly incorrect, at the same time that the imaginative turn of the expression is remarkably Hebraic. [Footnote 132] In the text, styled the received text, and which was fixed in the 16th century, many of these faults have disappeared, because it has borrowed from MSS. of then recent date. But now that biblical philosophy has mounted higher, we can discern how the copyists, one after the other, actuated by pious scruples, or thinking only to correct some error of their predecessors, have little by little effaced what appeared to them too great a departure from rules to have been written by an evangelist or an apostle. At the present day, these admitted irregularities are an element indispensible to every serious discussion respecting the nature and extent of the divine inspiration to be met with in the sacred volume.

[Footnote 132: Apocalypse i. 16; iii. 12; iv. 7; ix. 13 & 14; xiv. 12; xvi. 13; xx. 2, &c.]

THE END.

CPSIA information can be obtained
at www.ICGtesting.com
Printed in the USA
LVHW041011020323
740706LV00008B/953